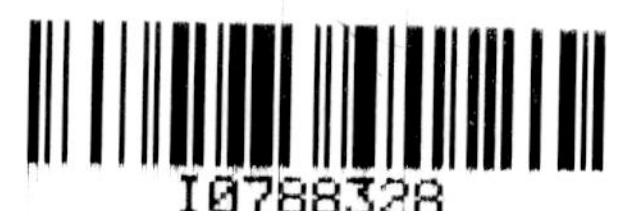

Coloring book for adults and kids amazing donkey image for design

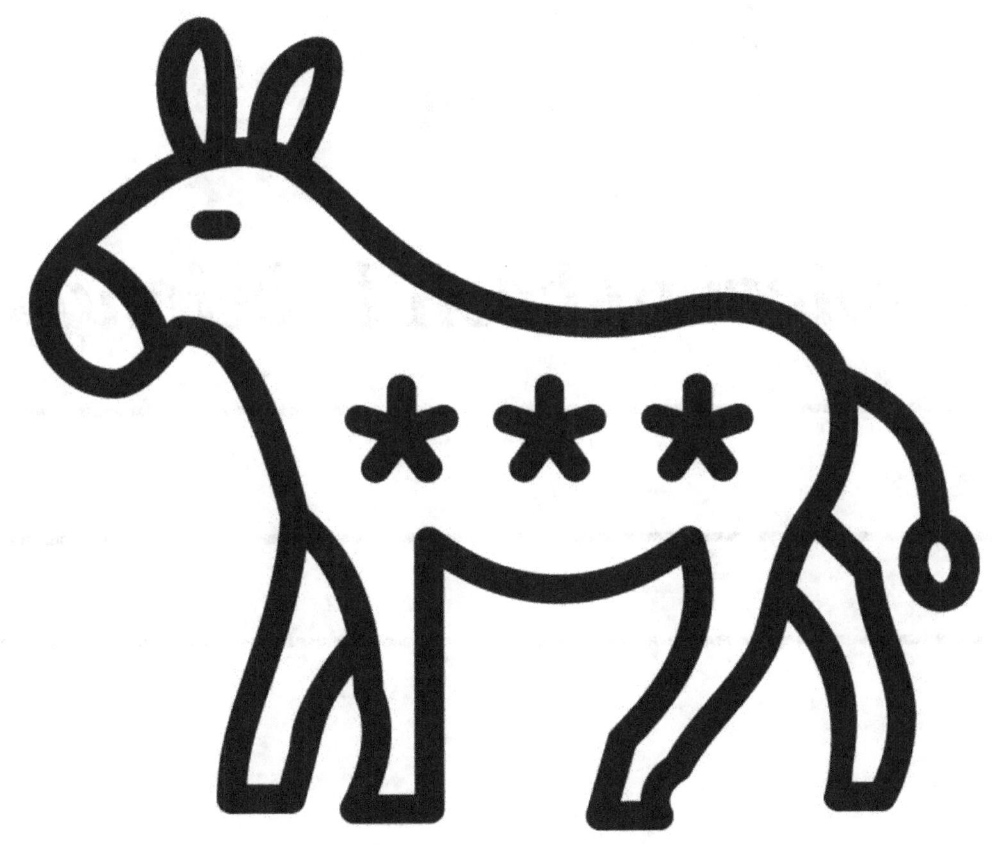

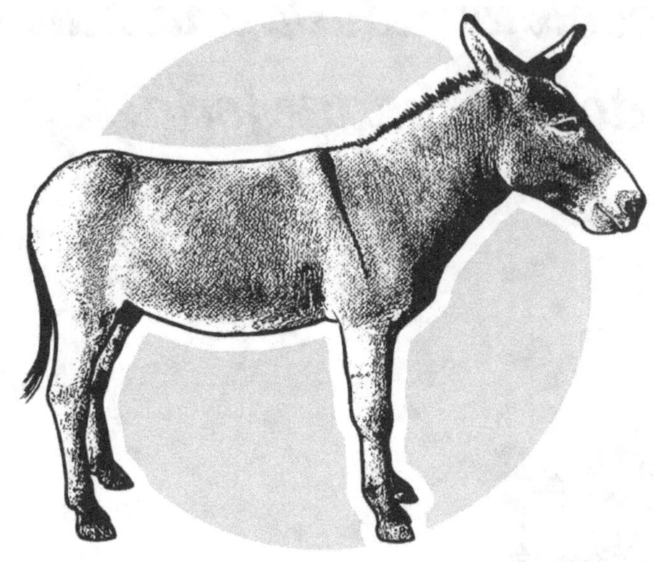

This coloring book is belongs to

____

____

____

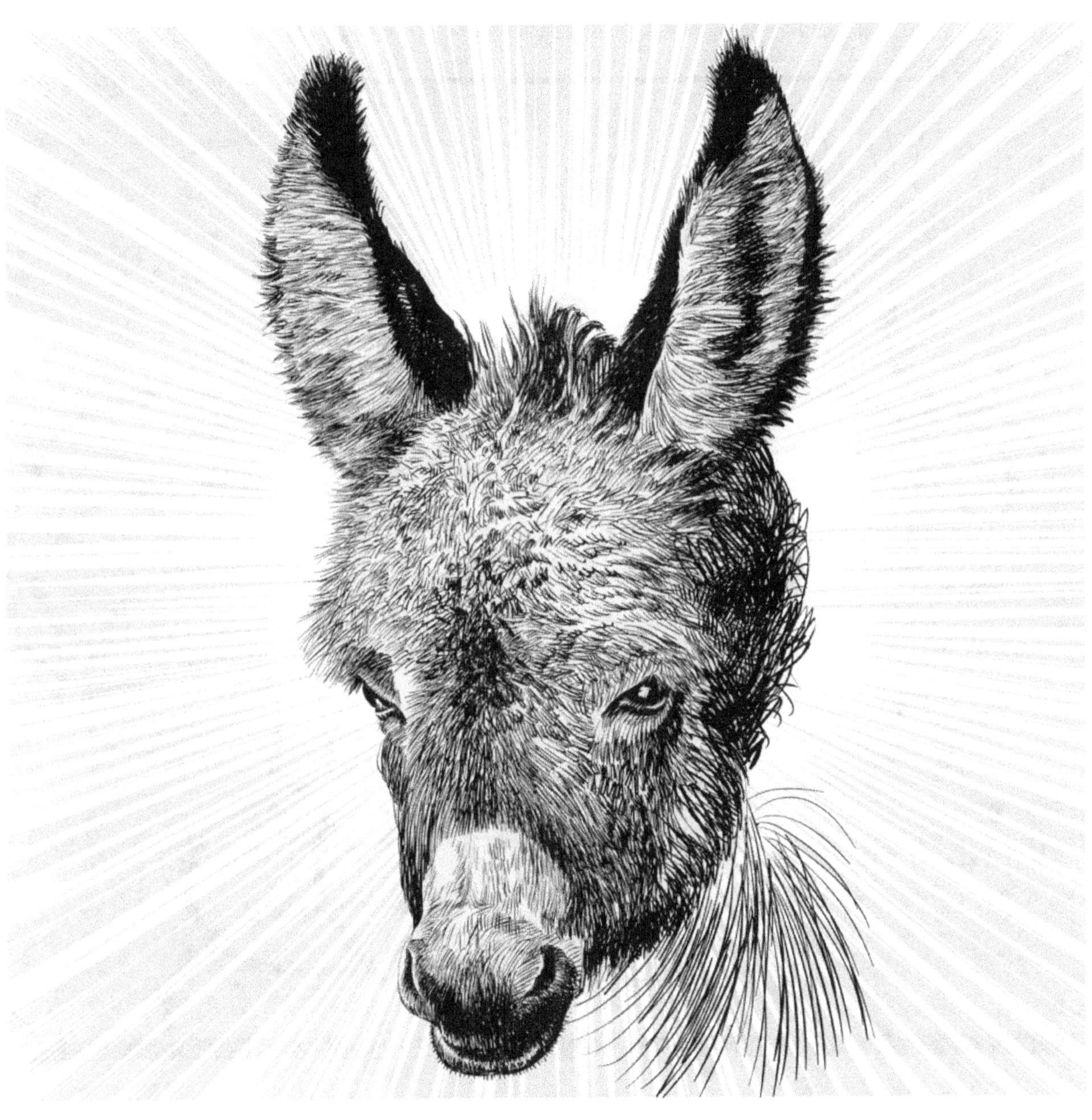

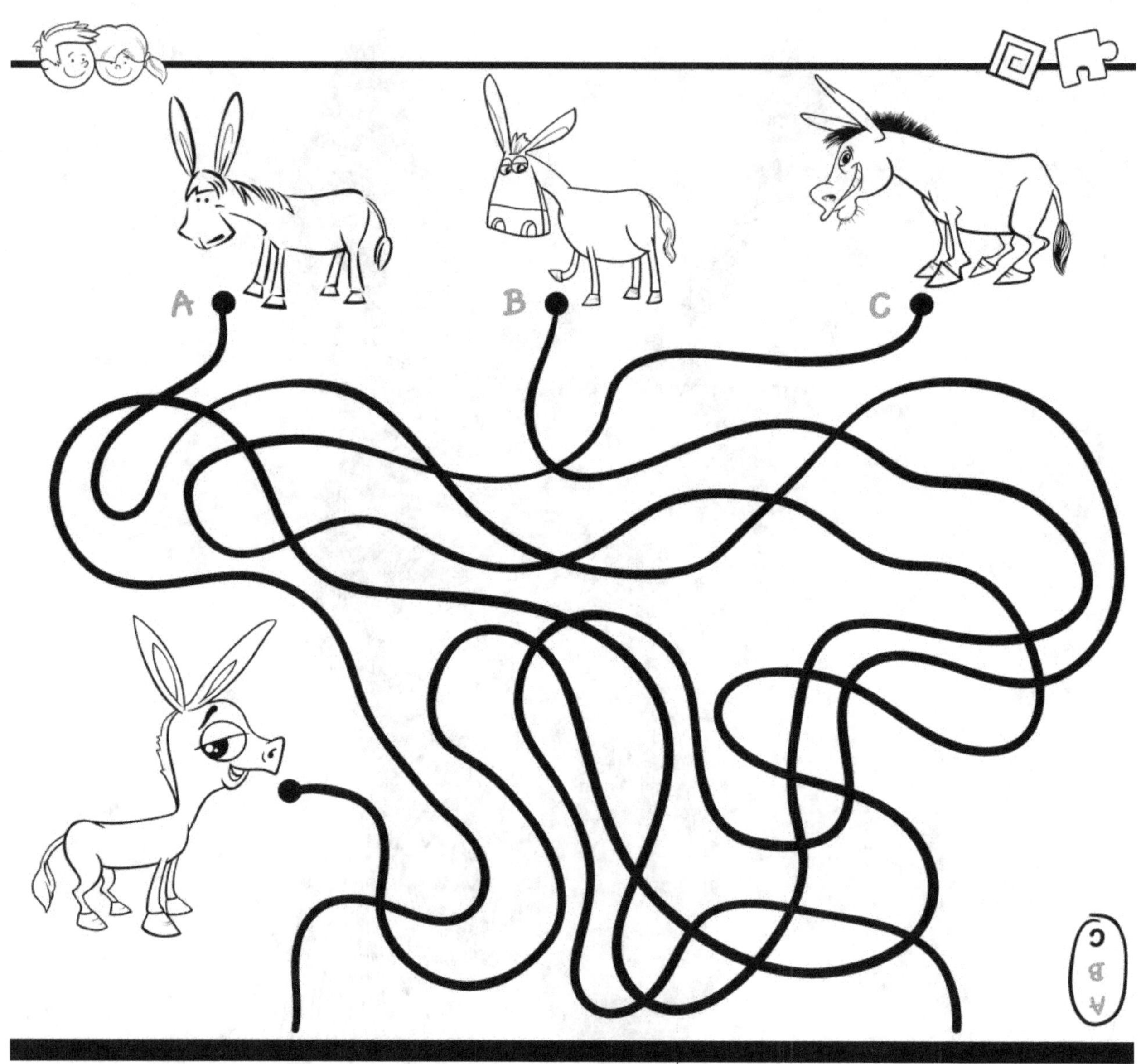

A
B
C

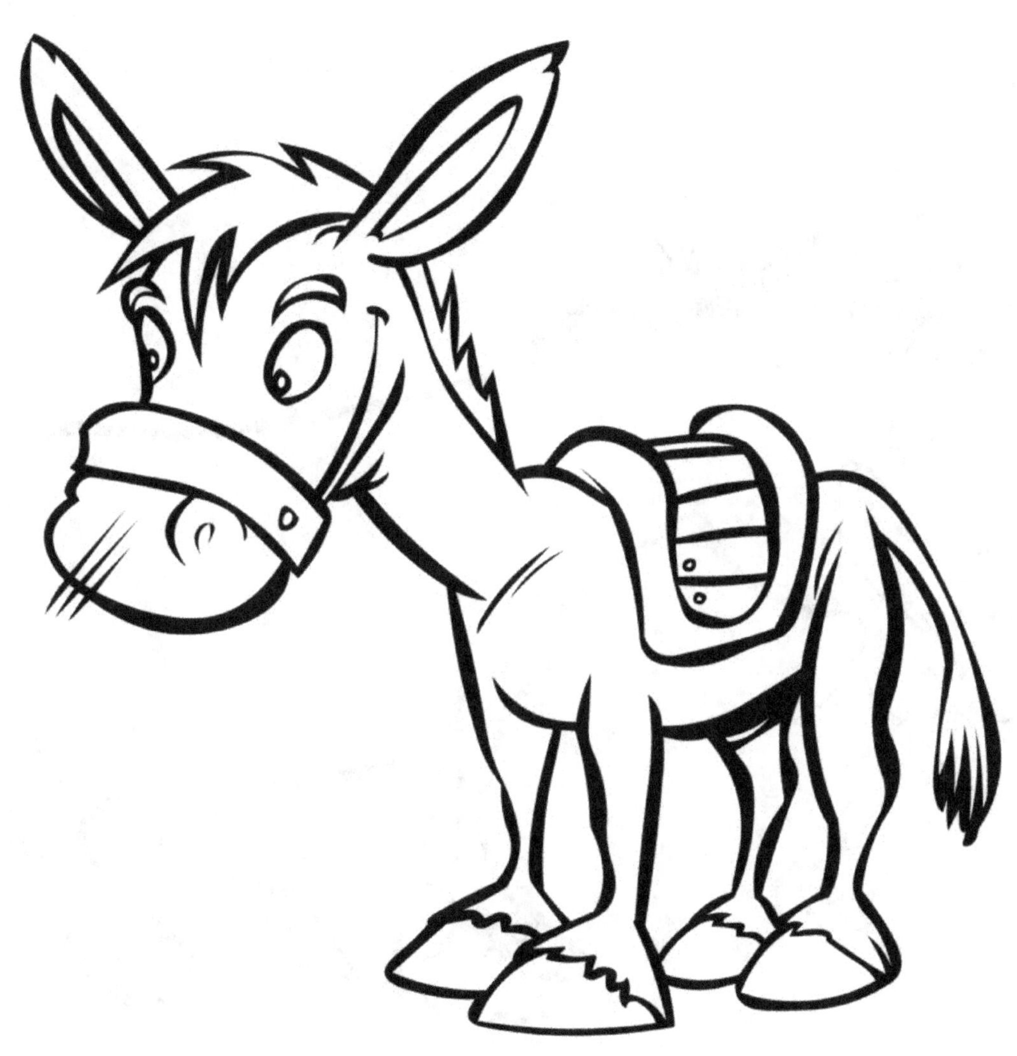

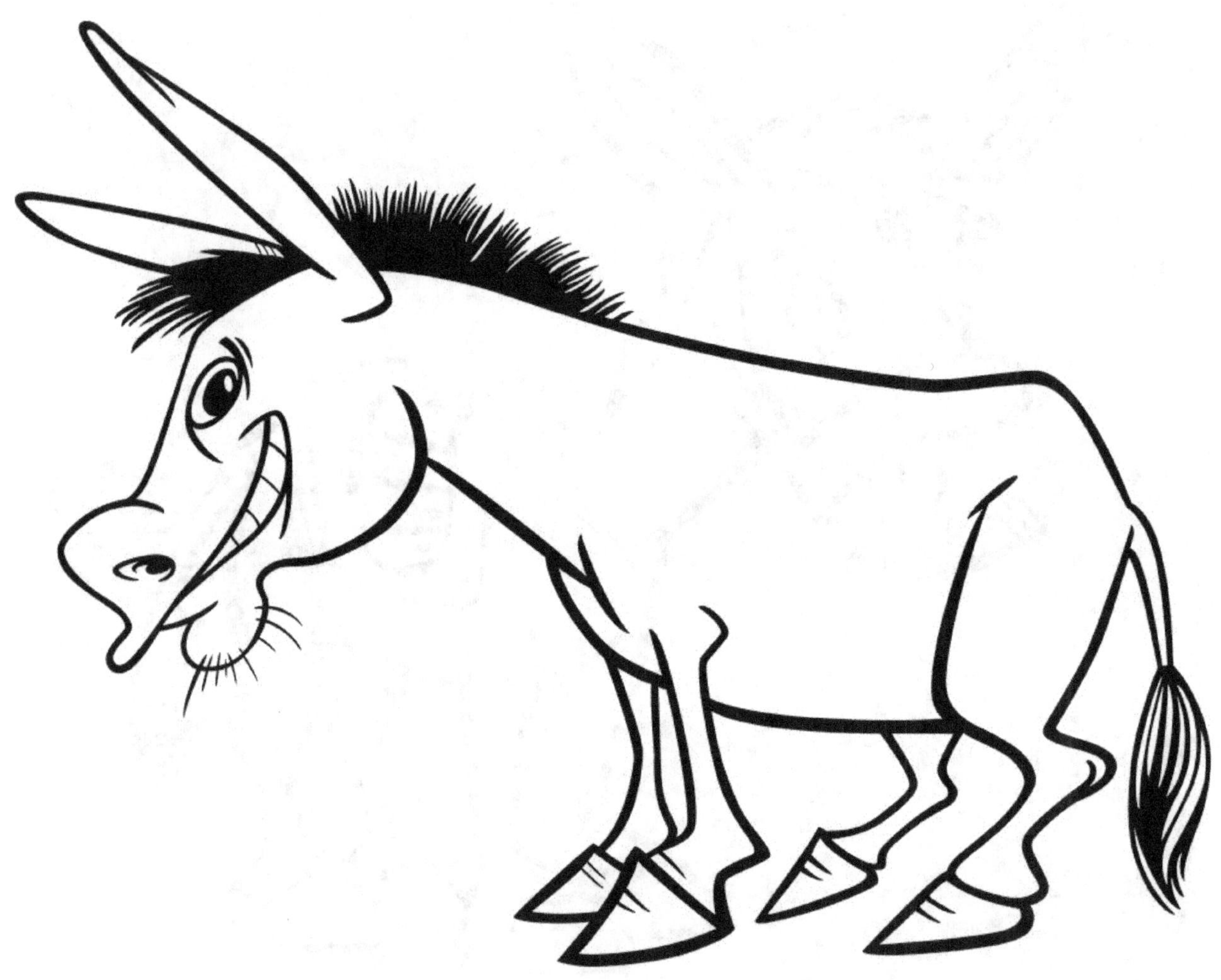

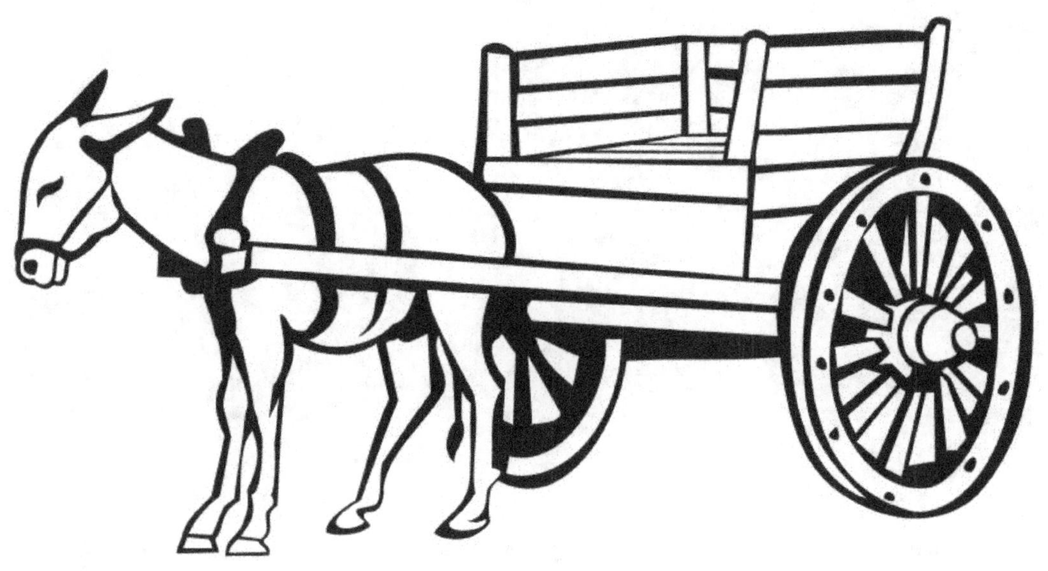

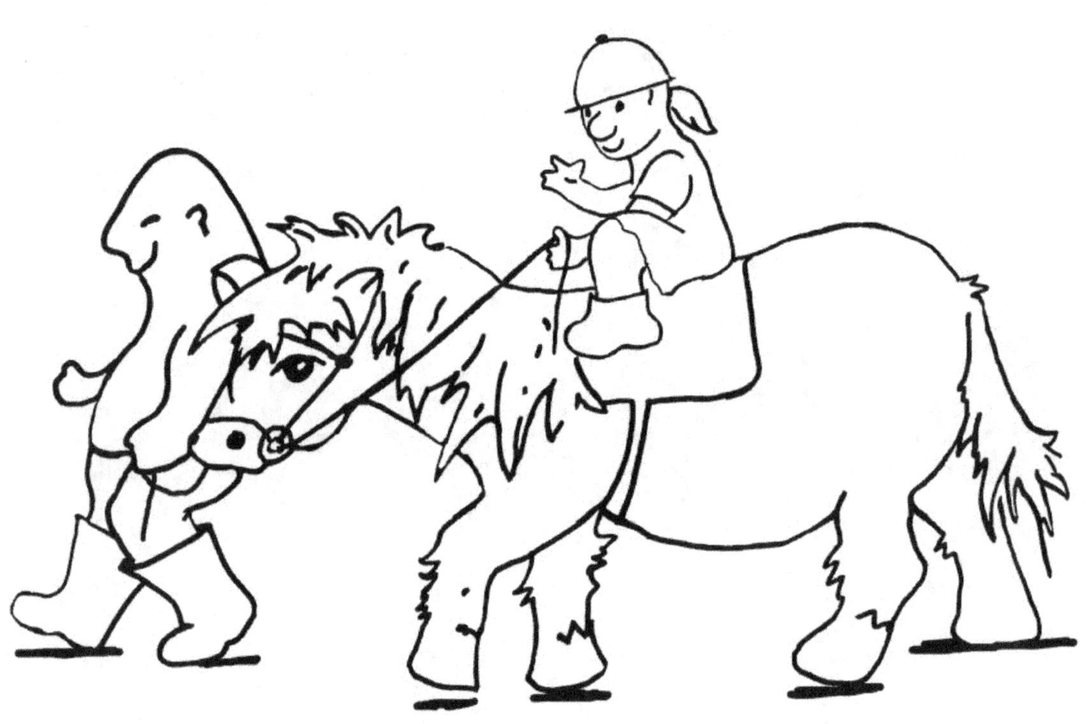

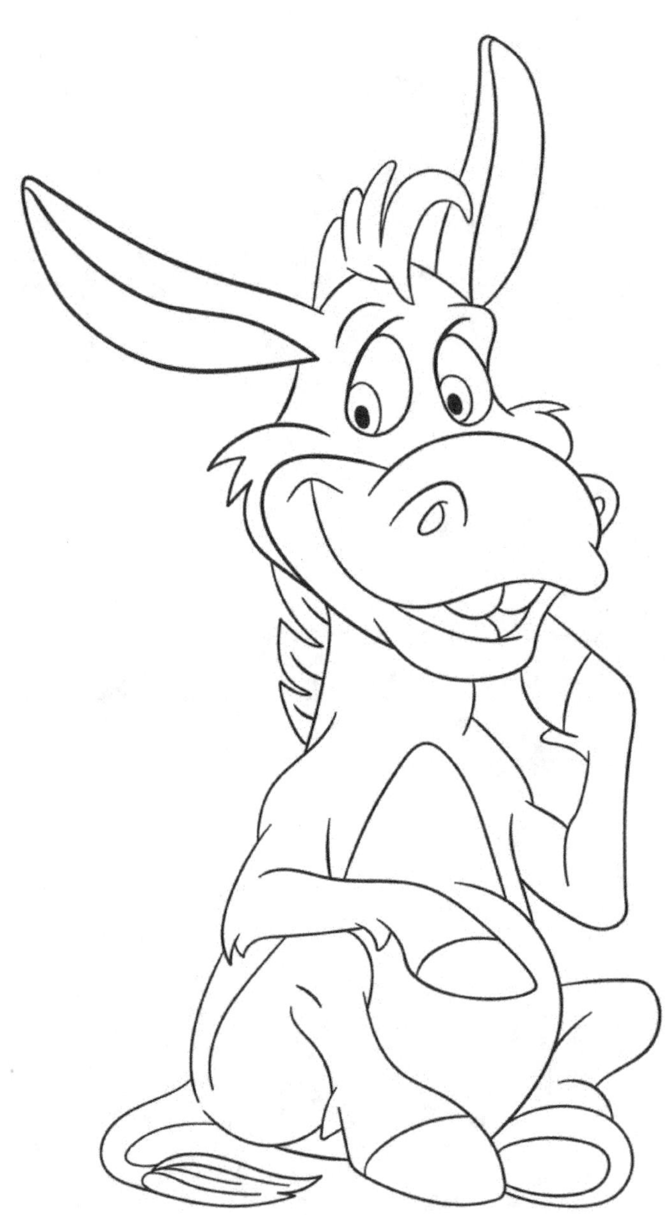

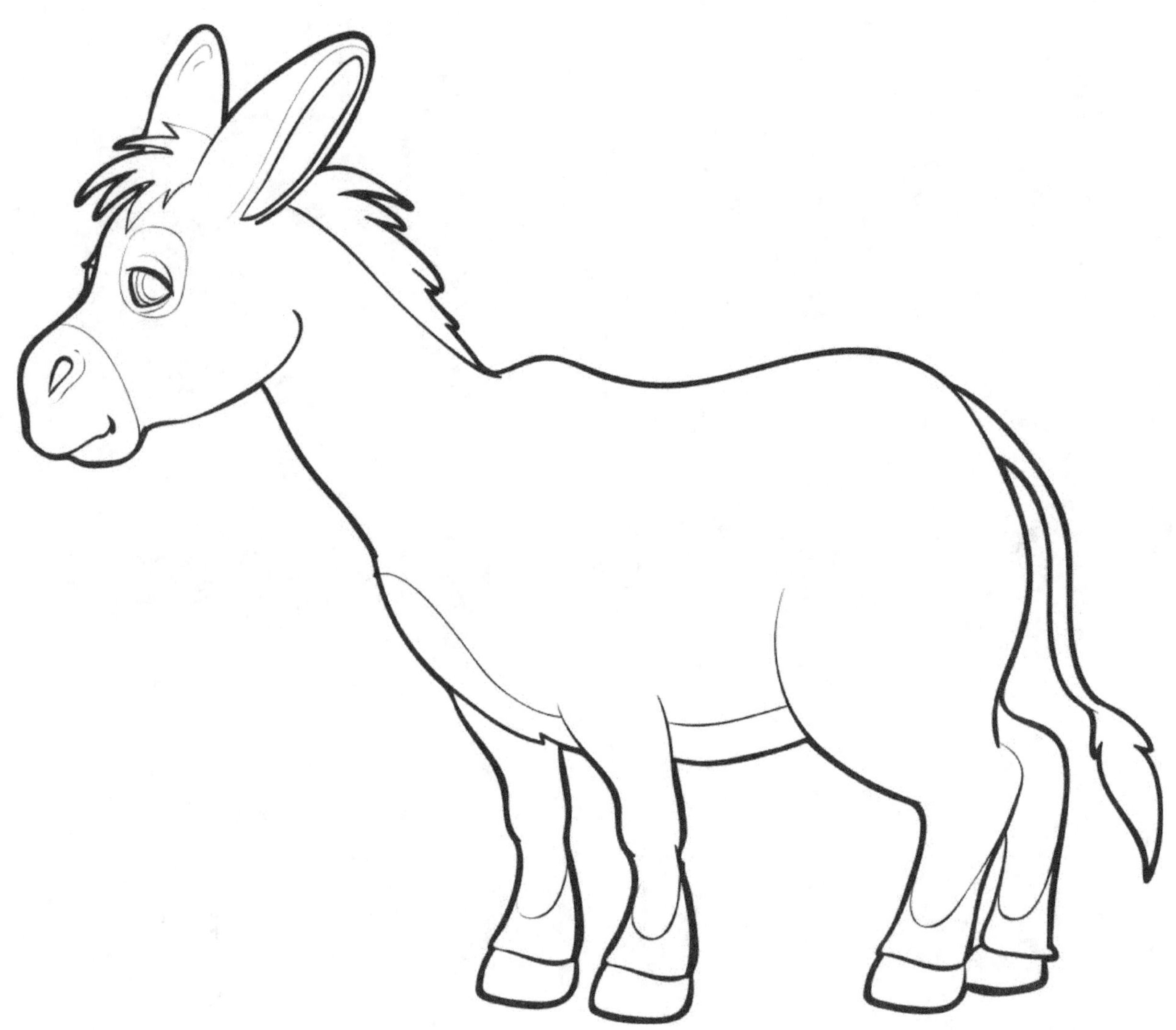

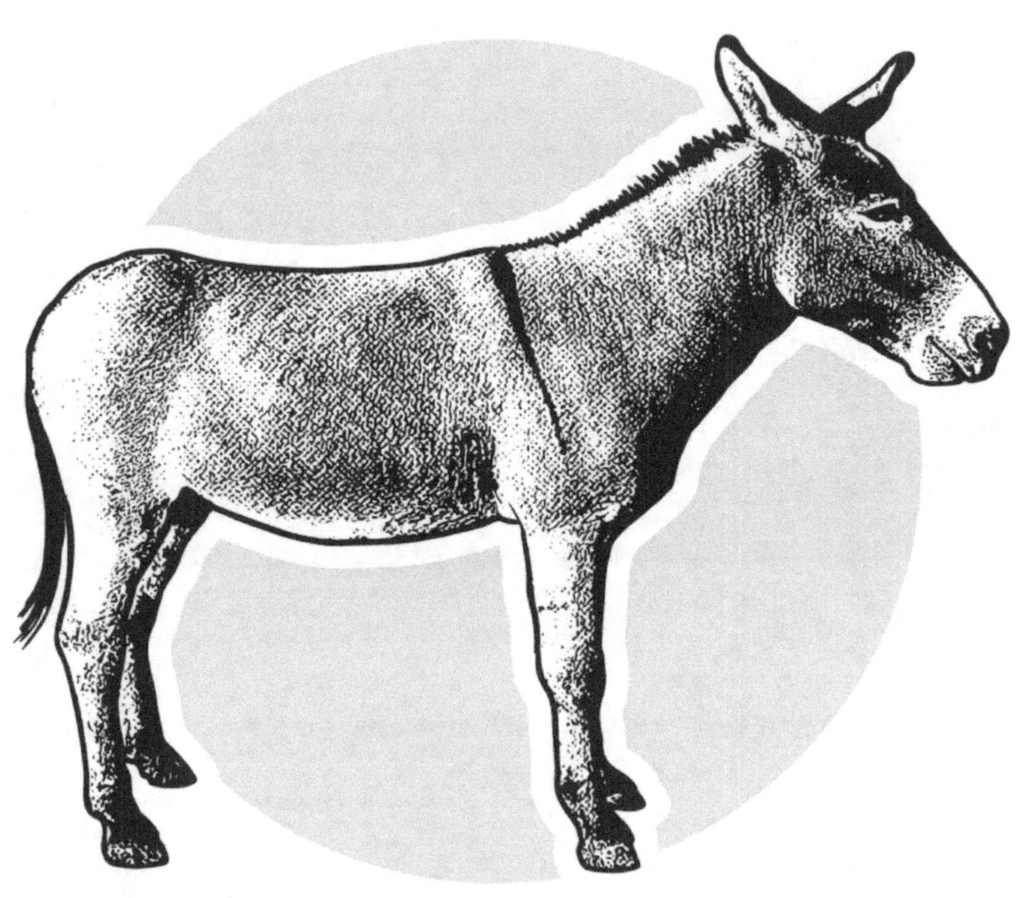

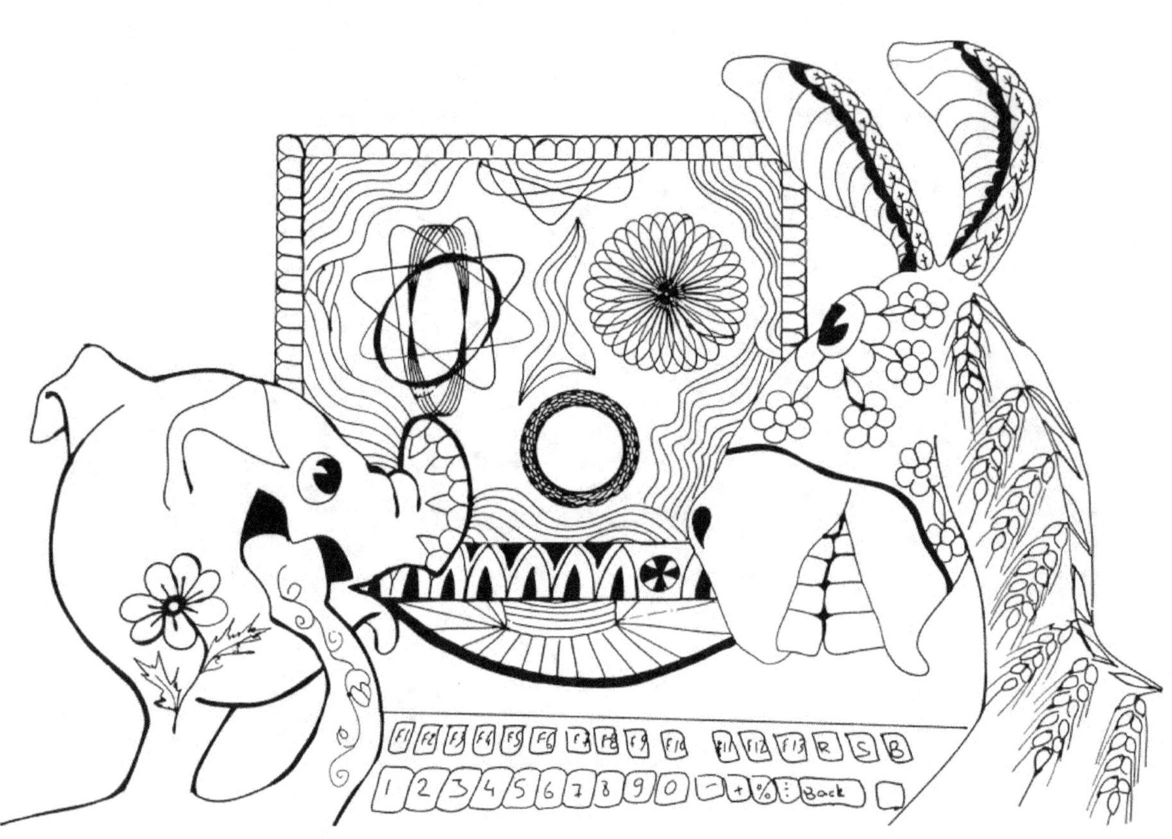

F1 F2 F3 F4 F5 F6 F7 F8 F9 F10 F11 F12 F13 R S B
1 2 3 4 5 6 7 8 9 0 - + % : Back

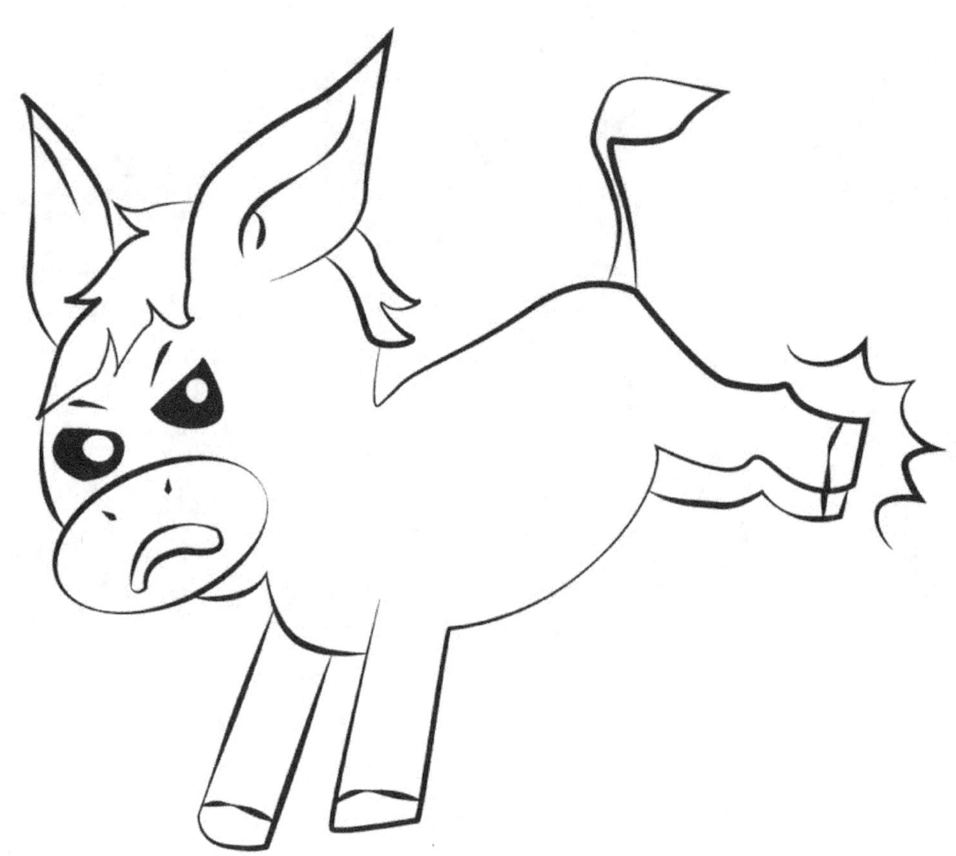

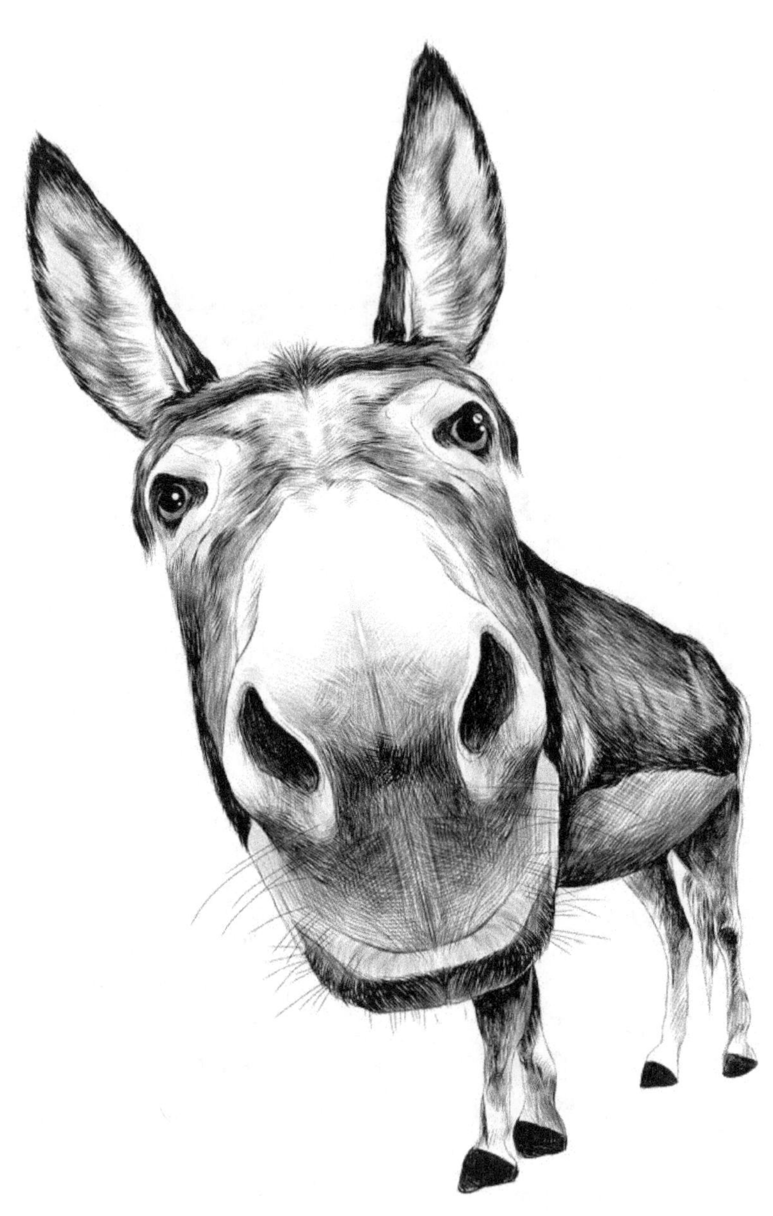

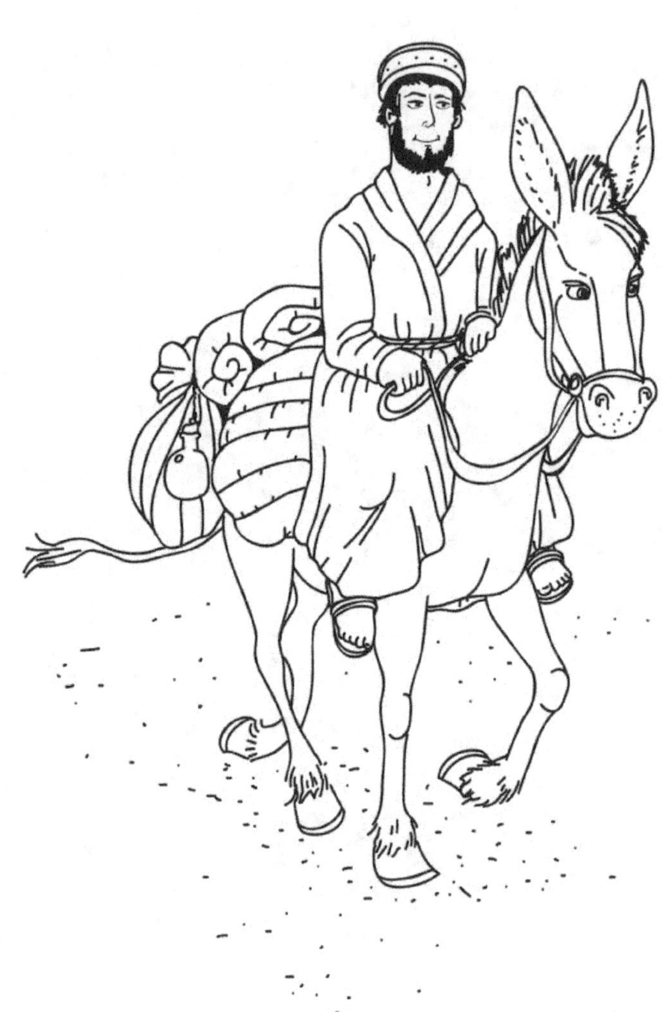

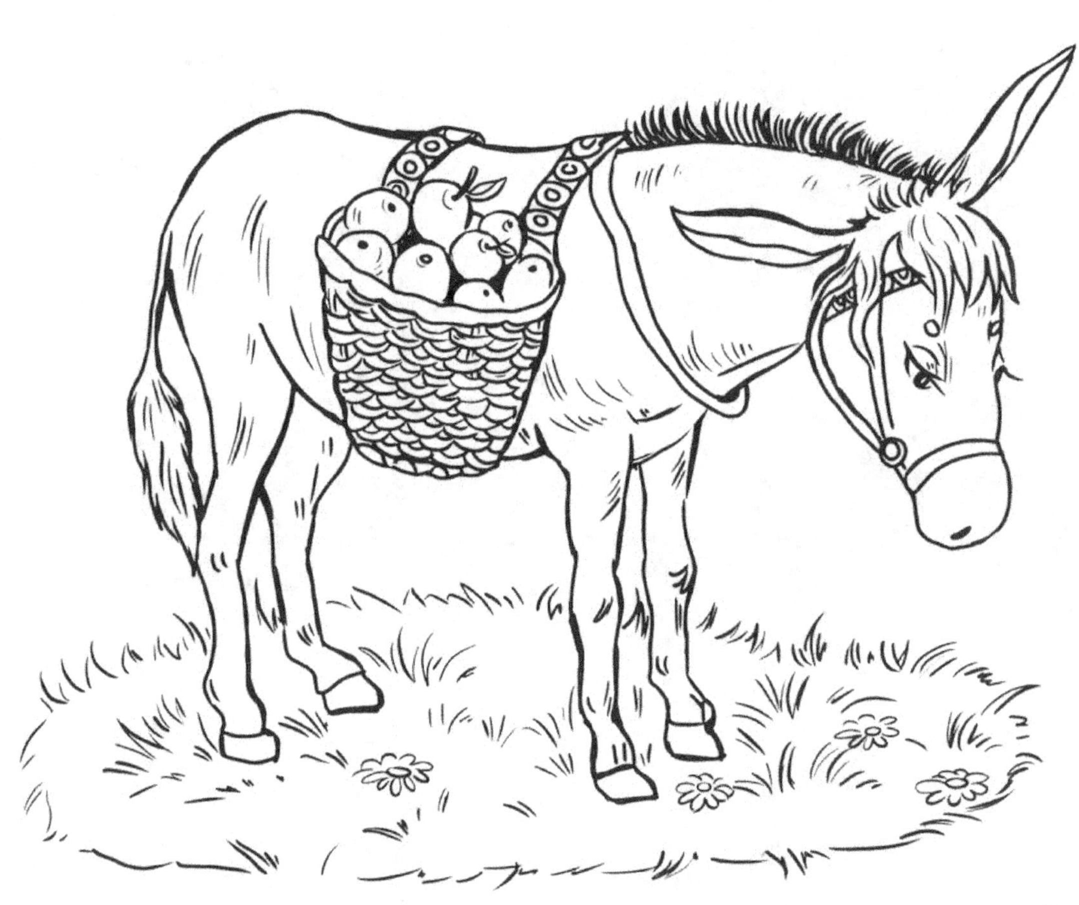

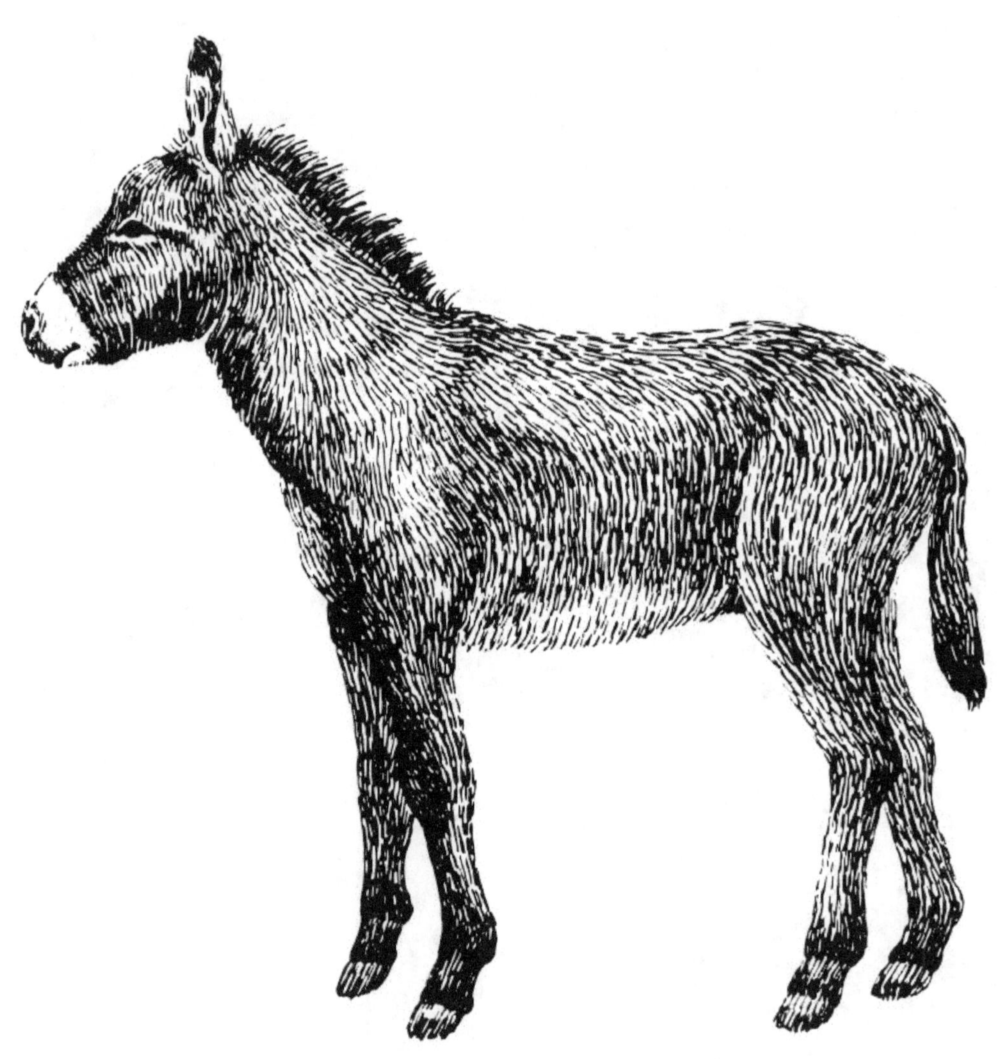

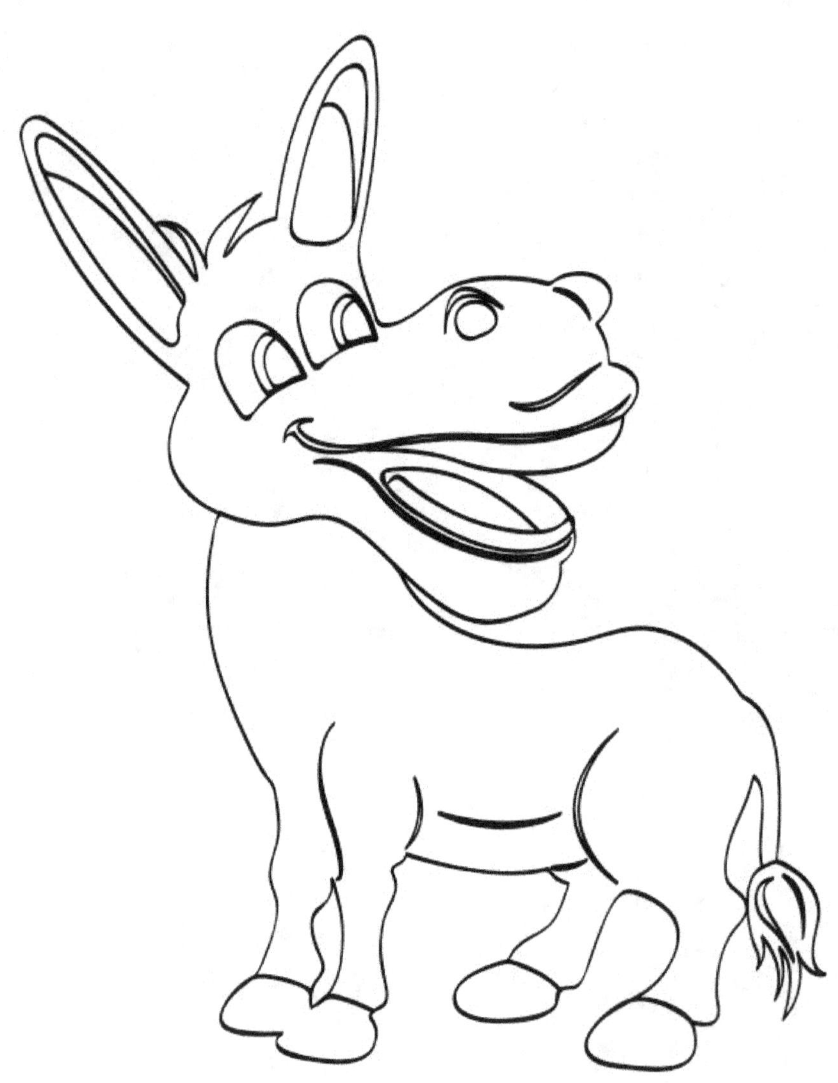

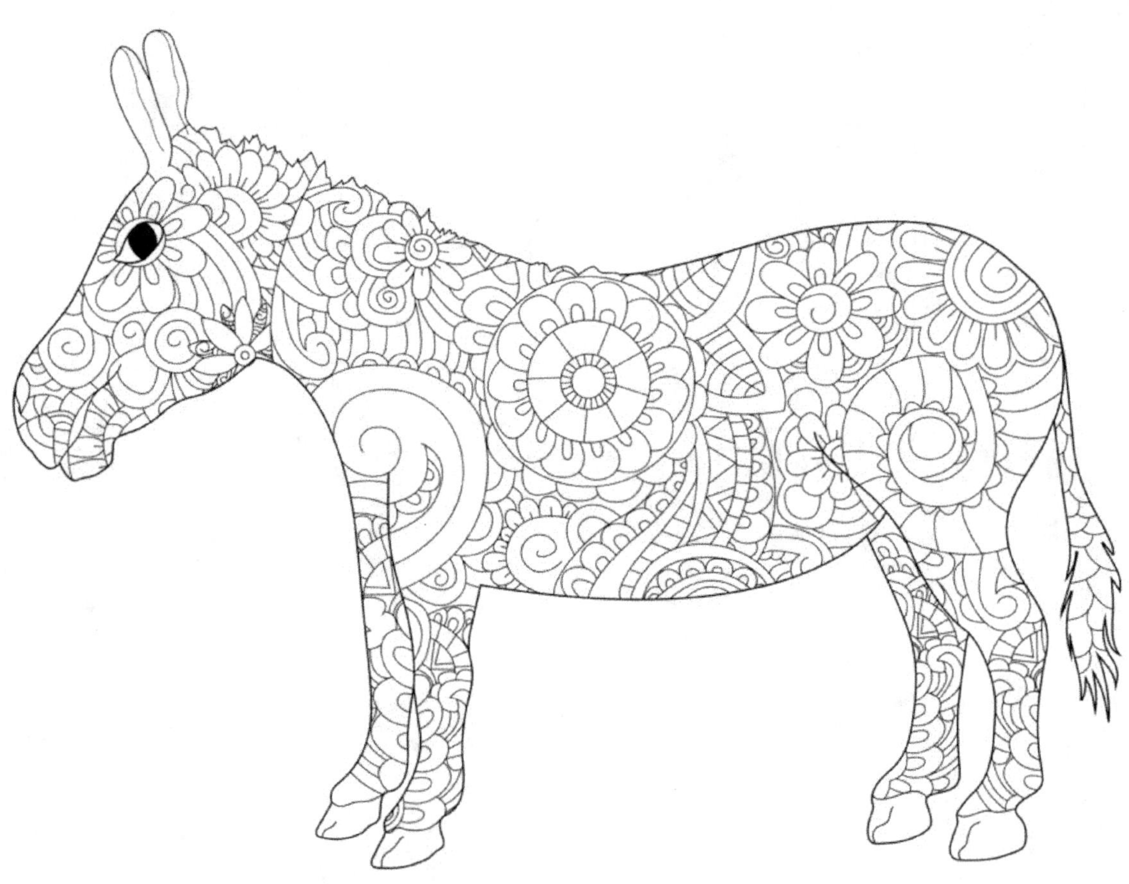

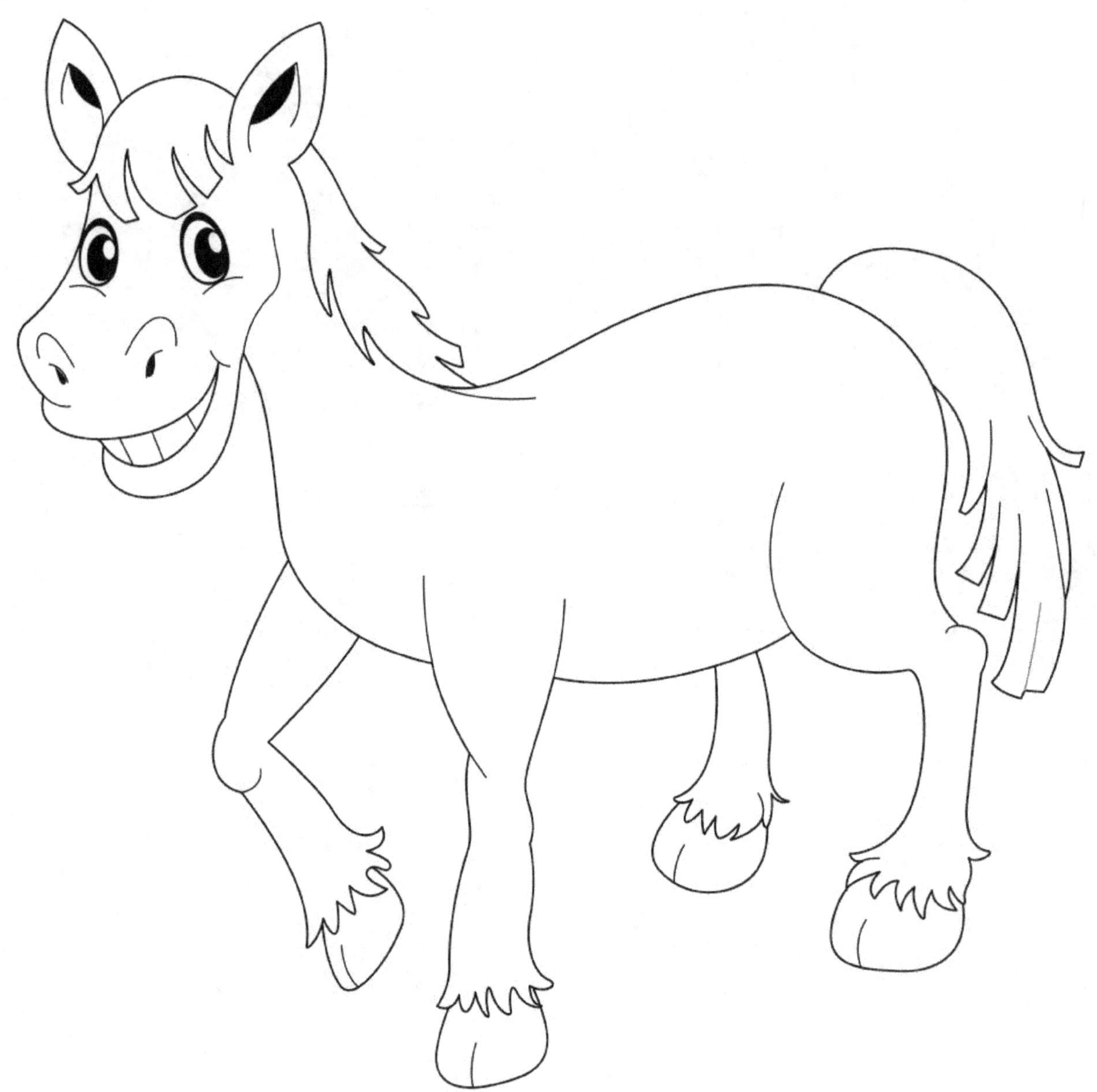

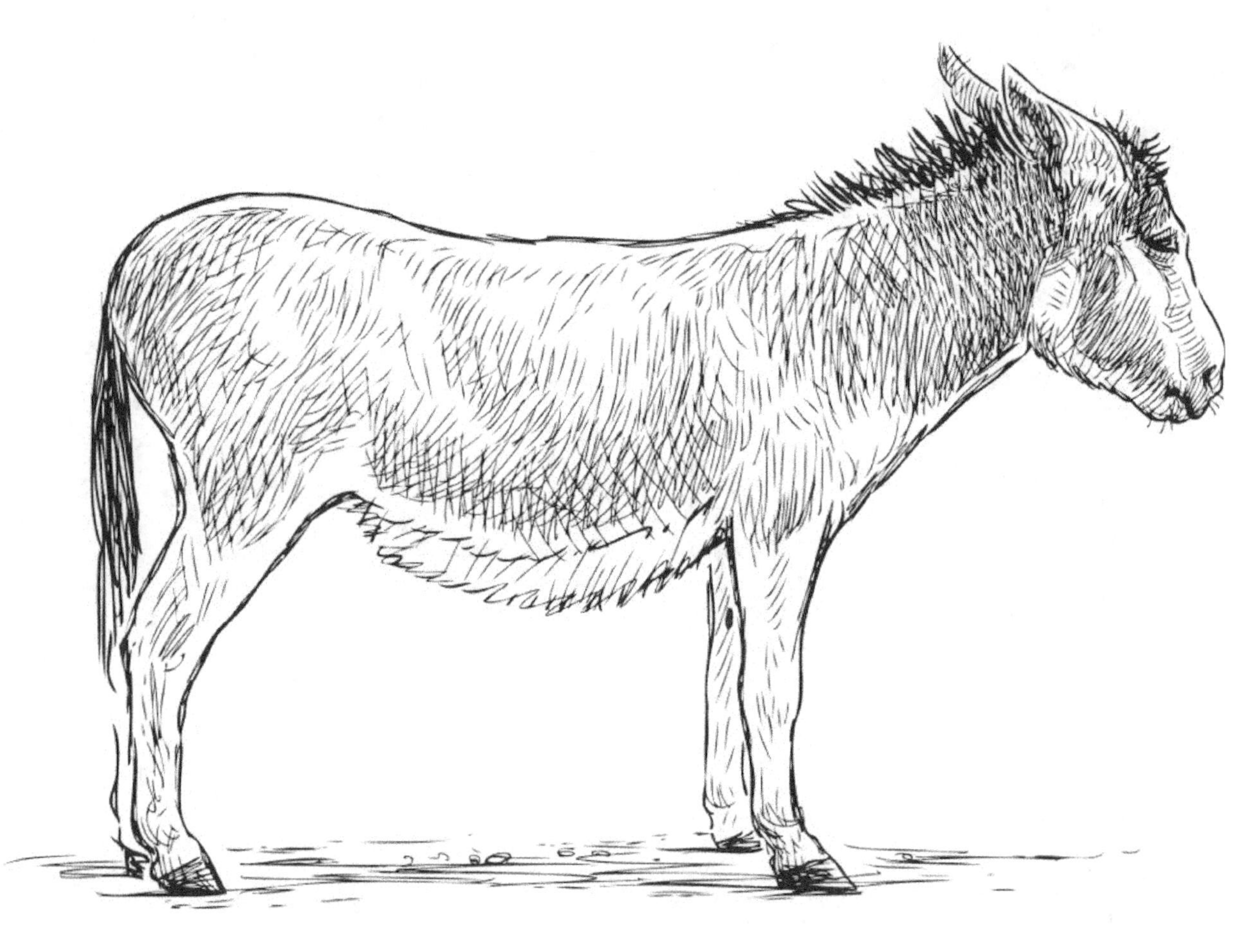

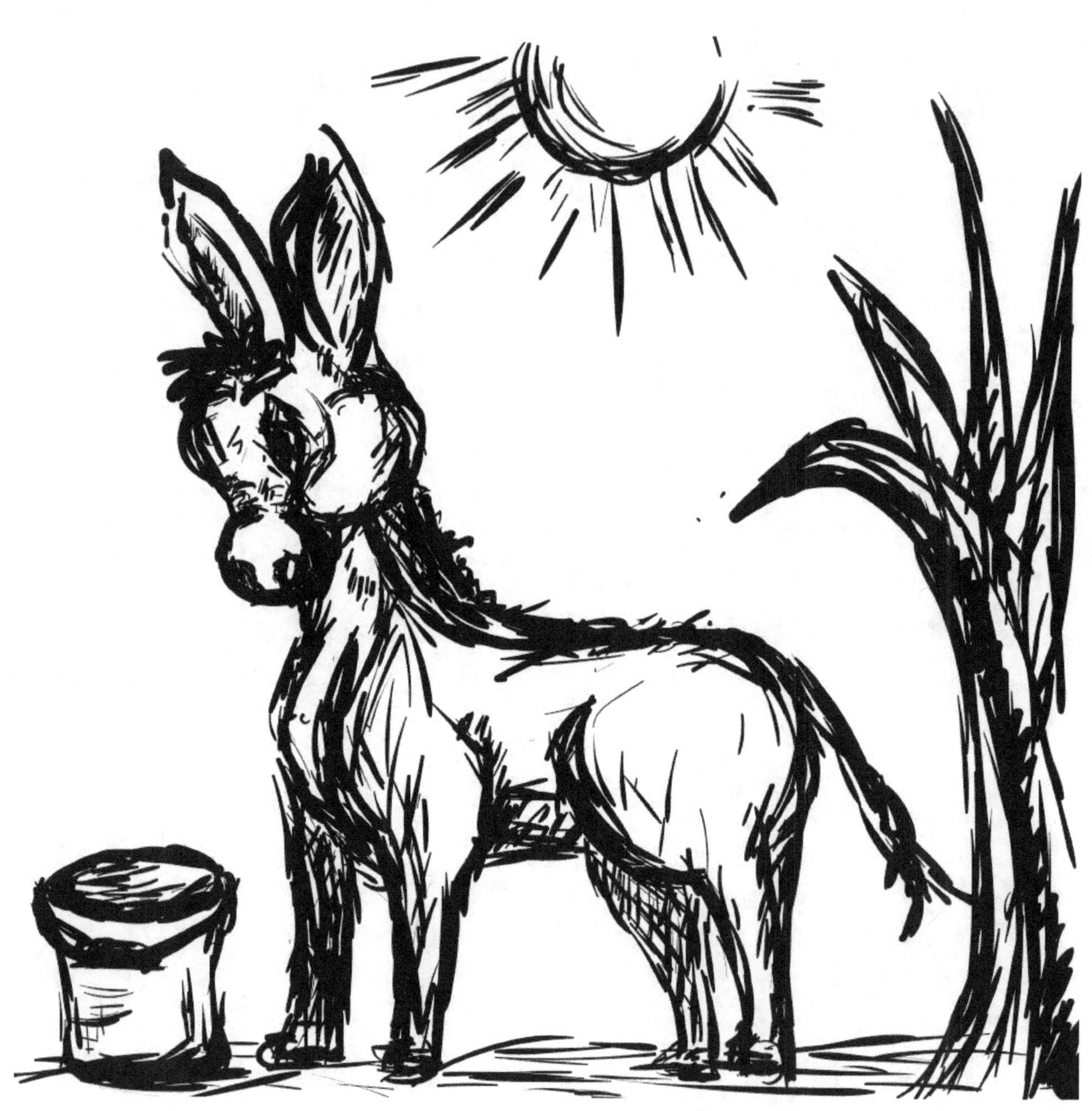

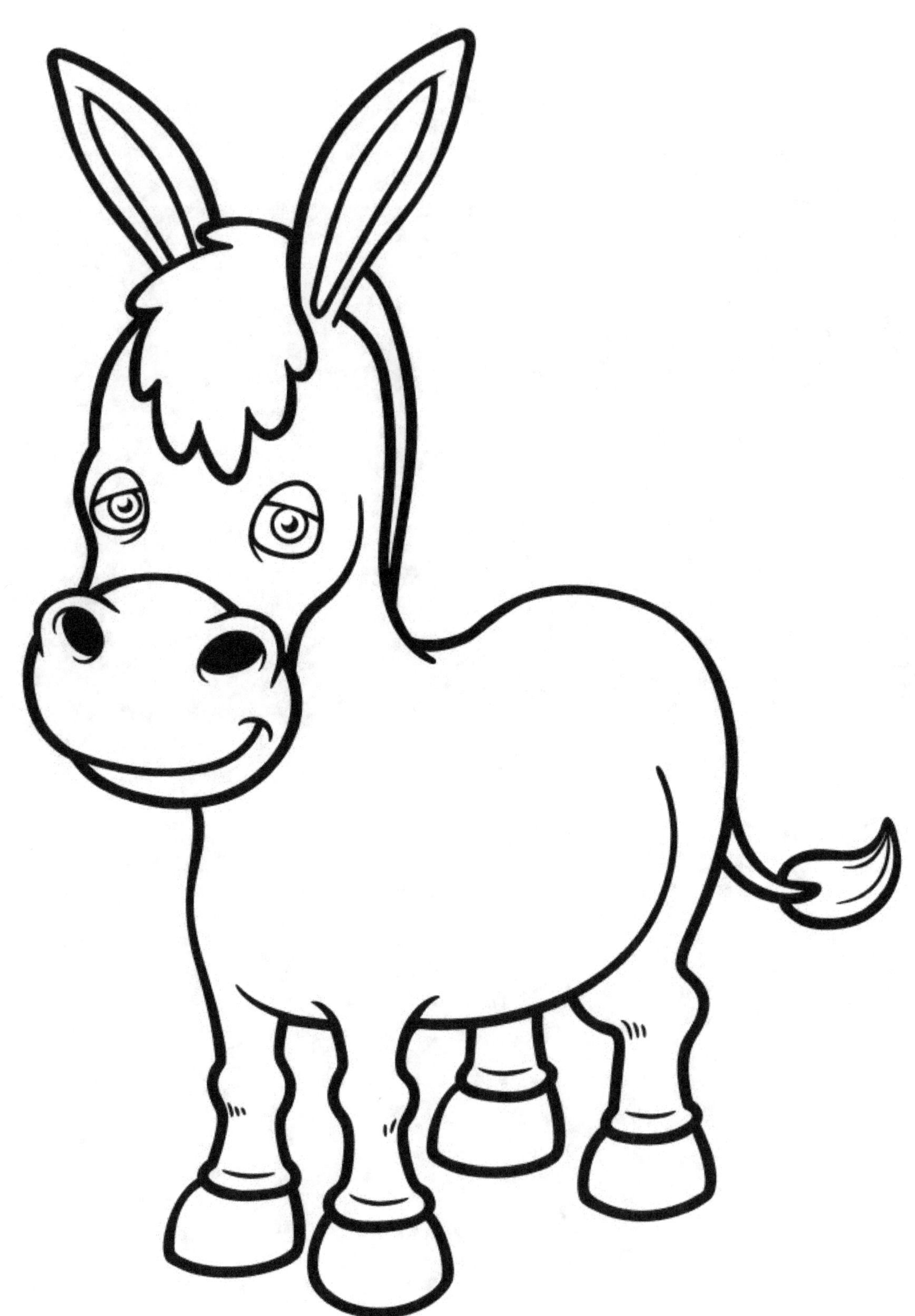

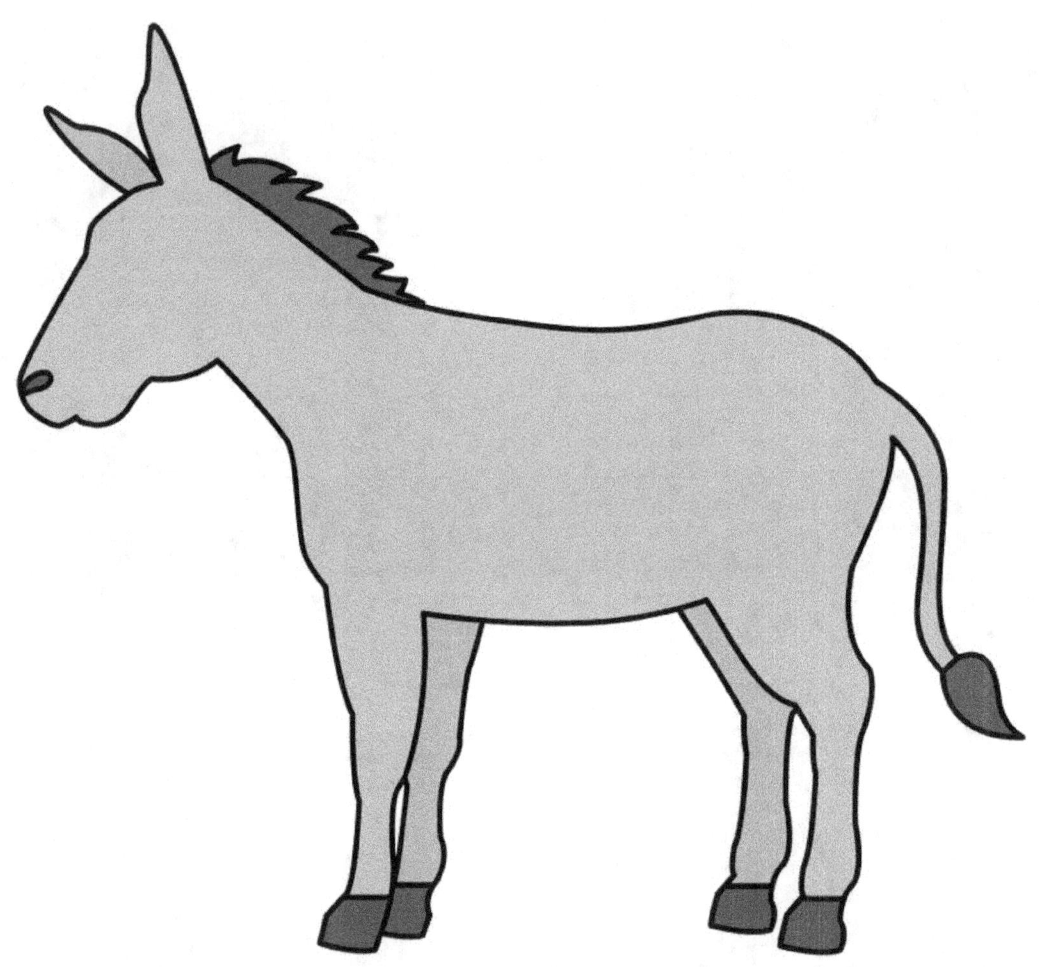

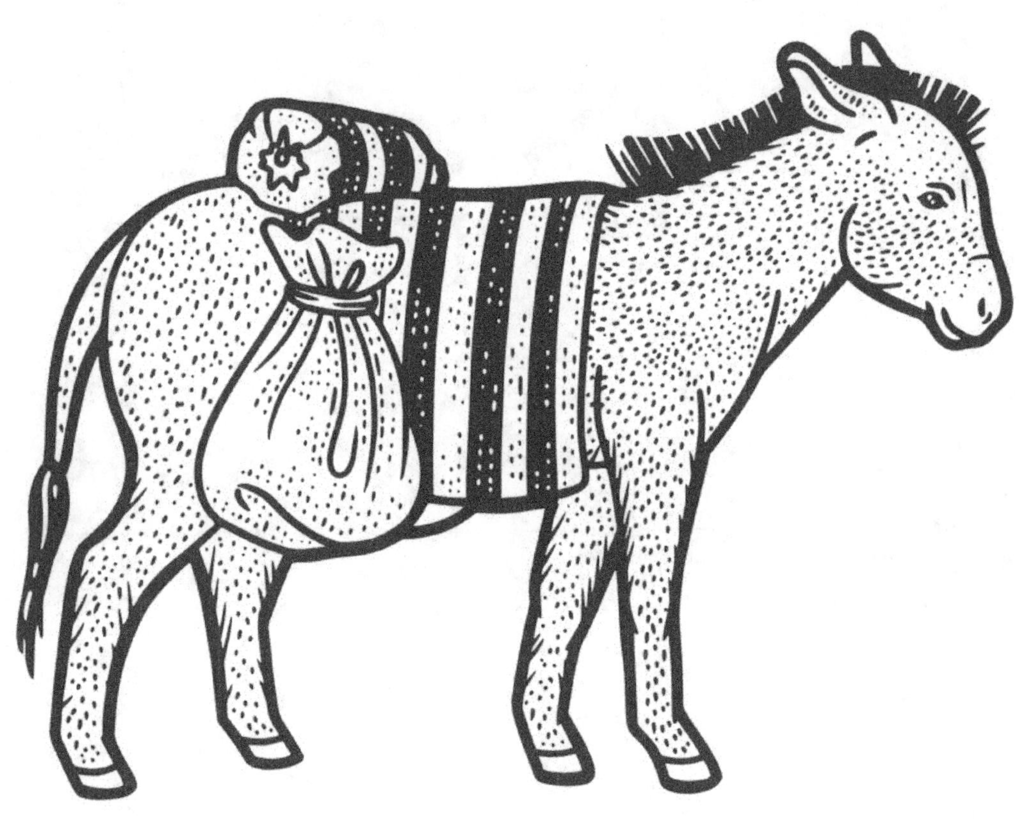

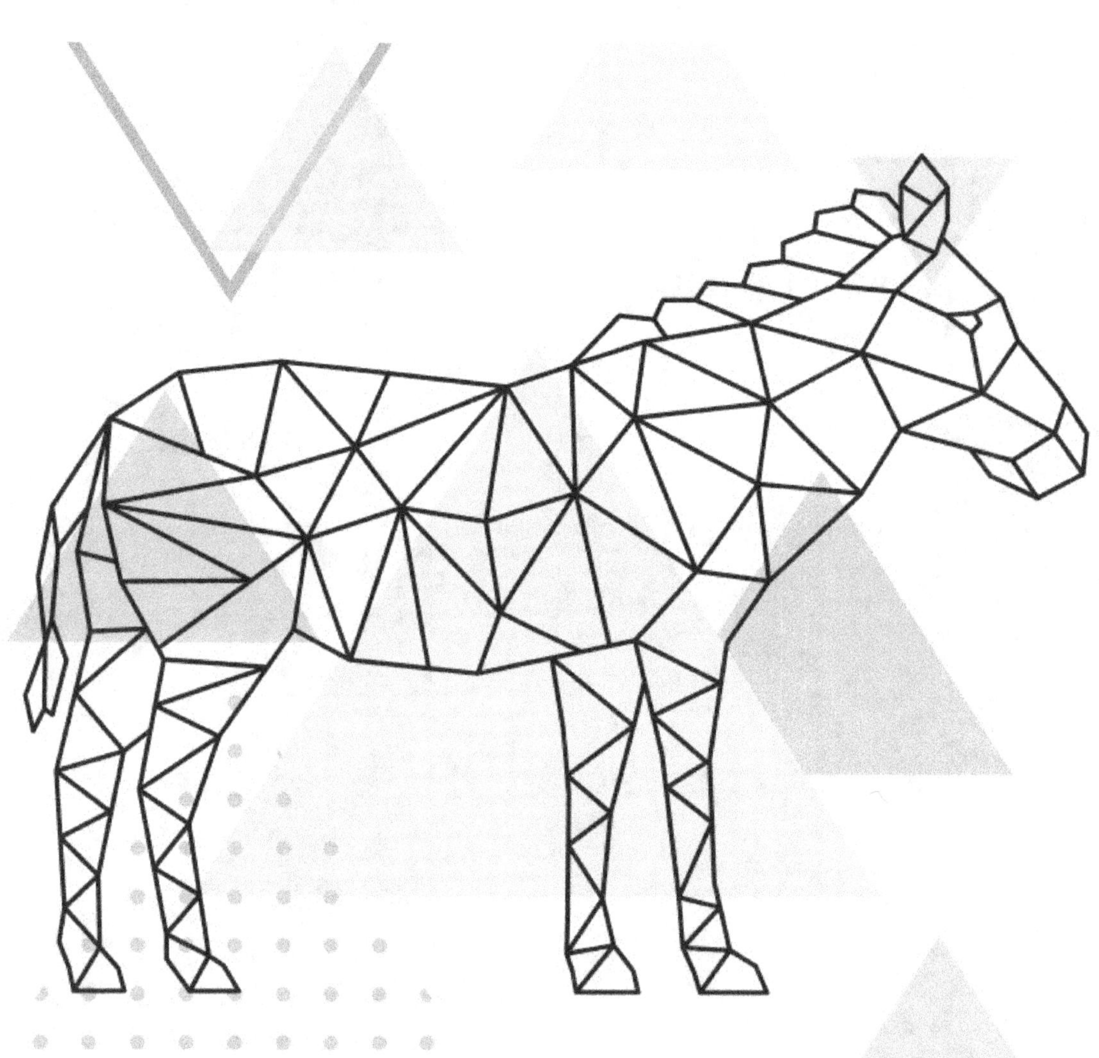

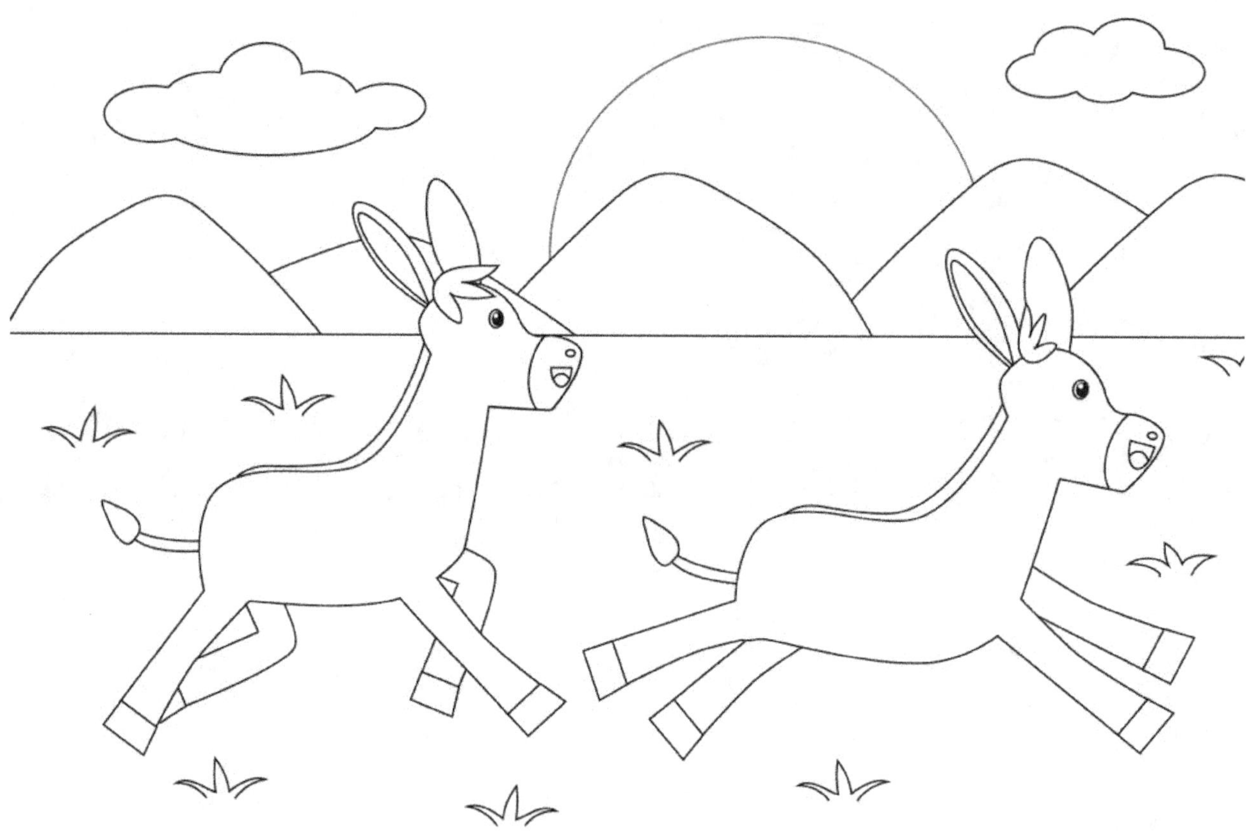

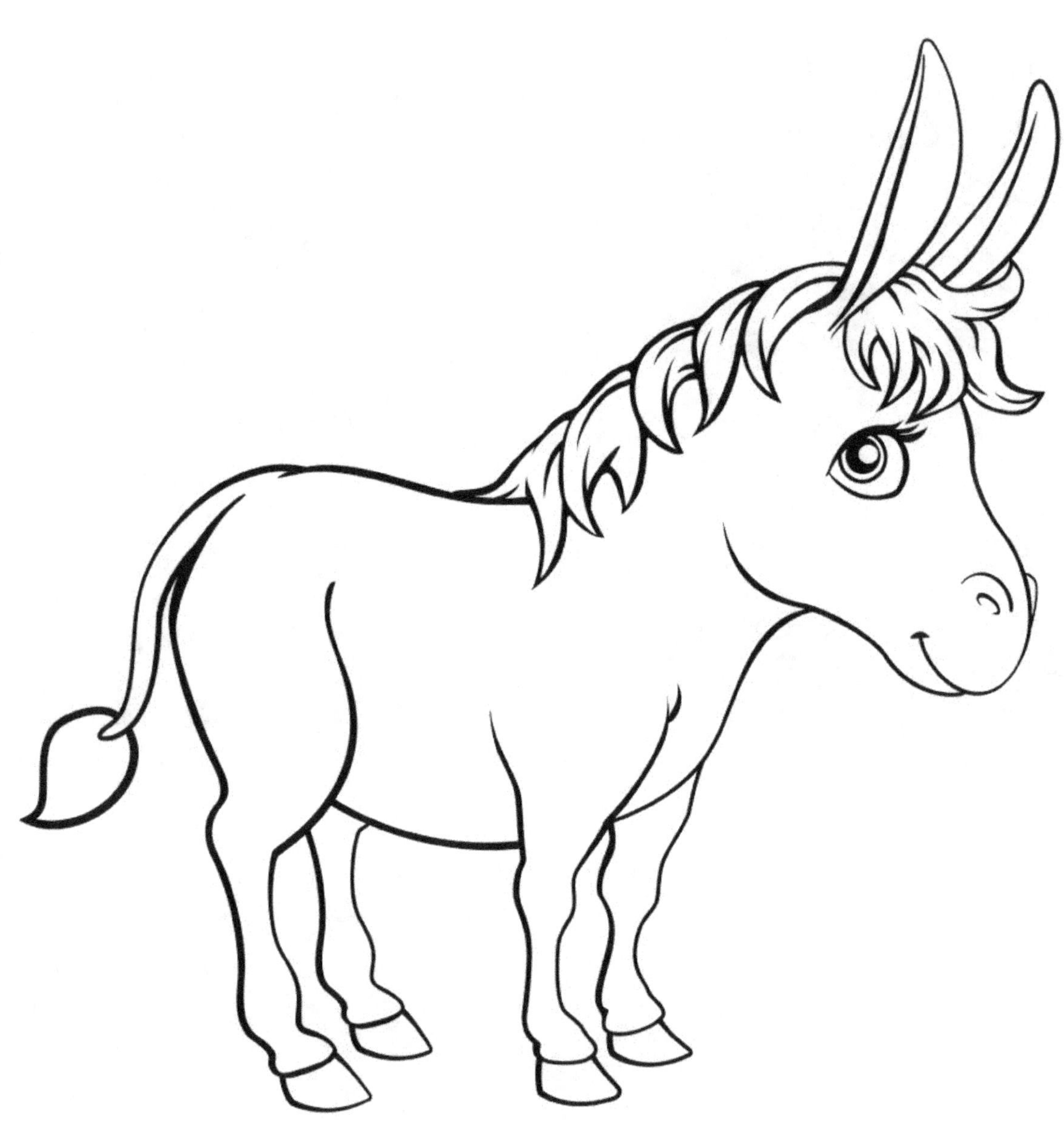

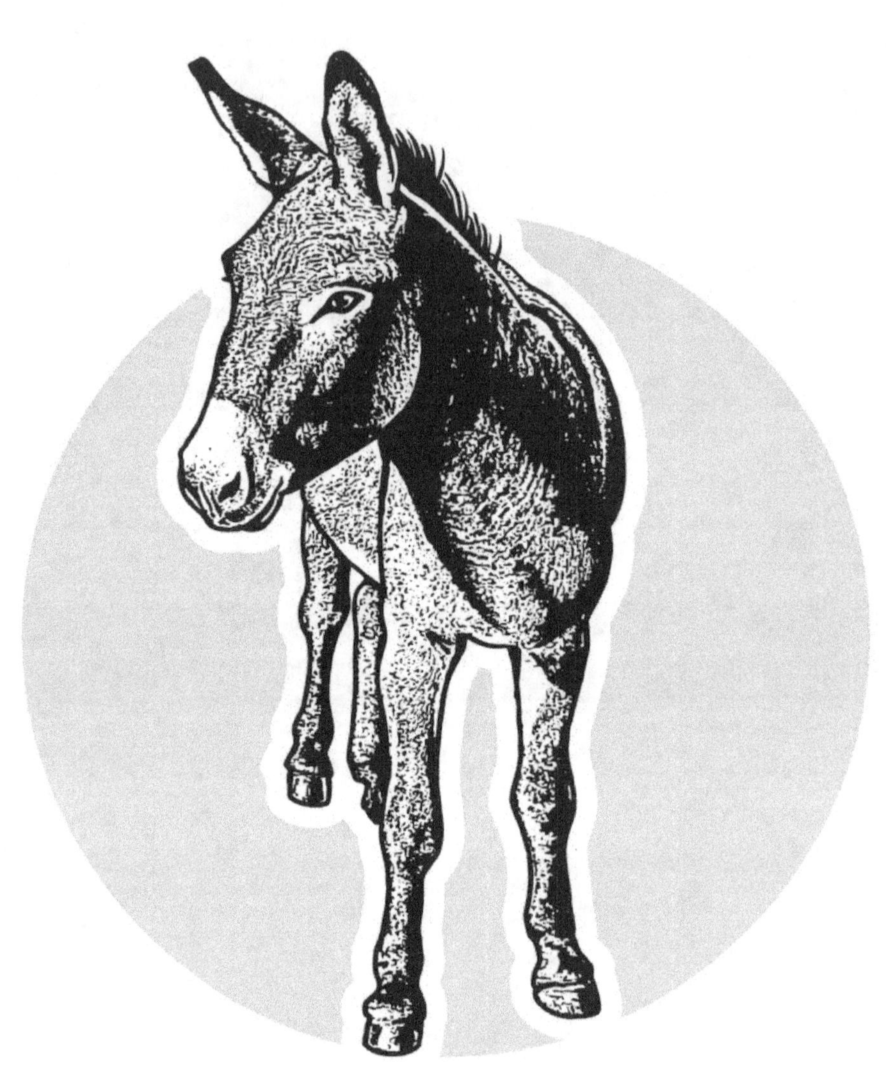

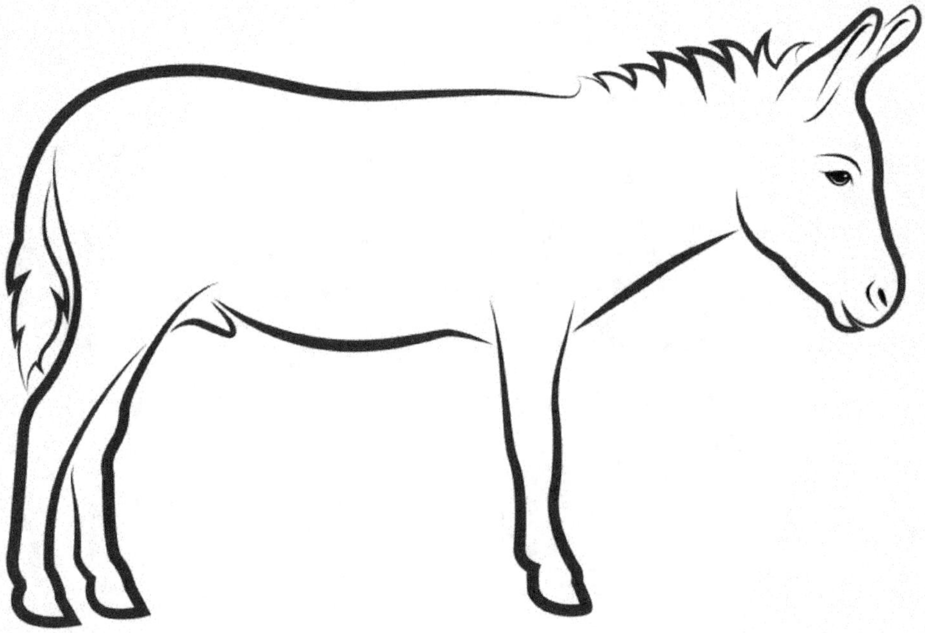

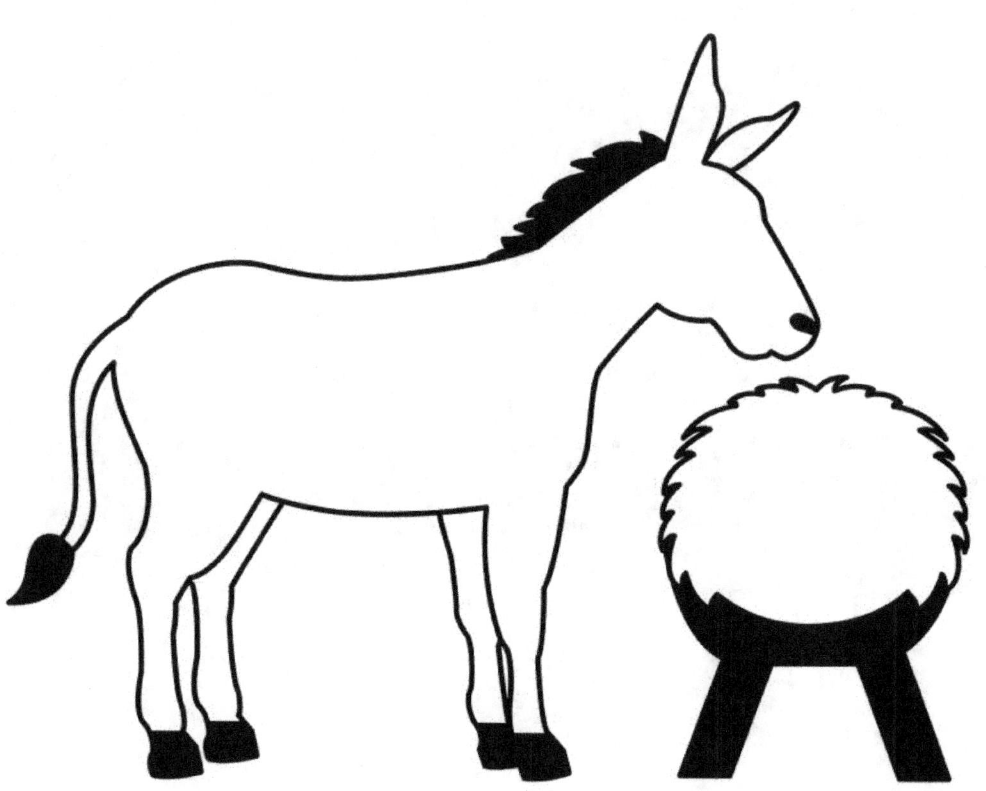

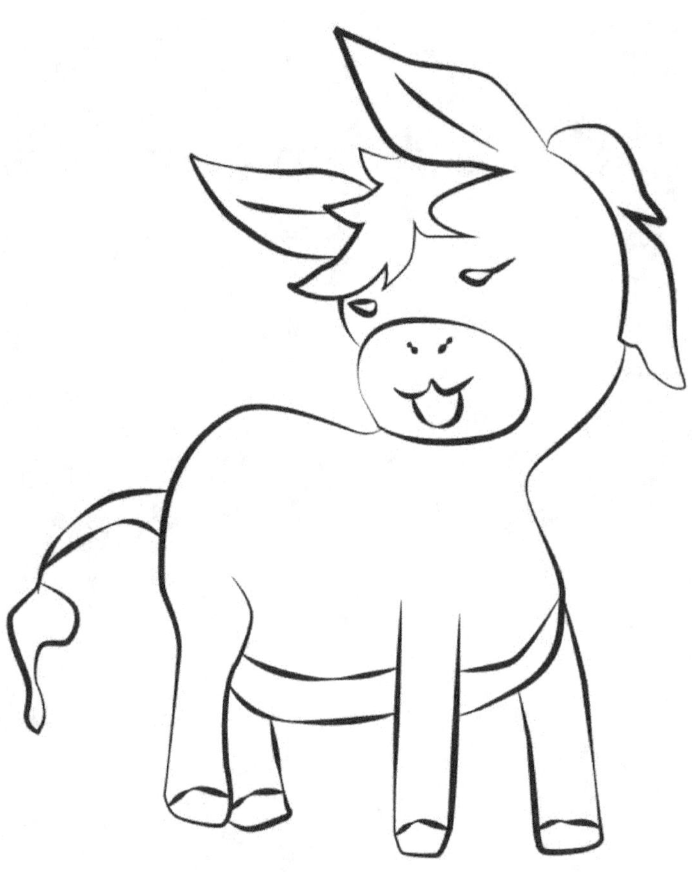

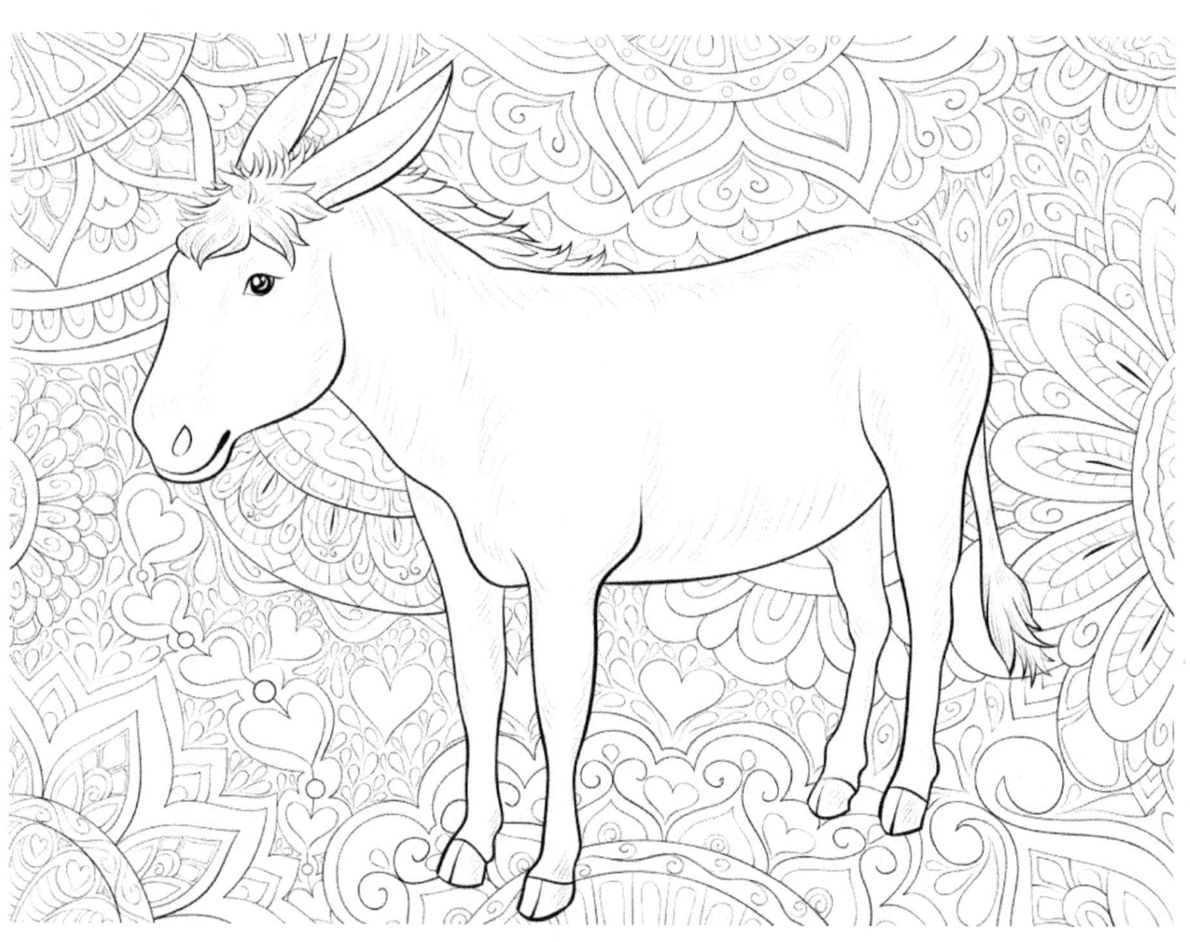

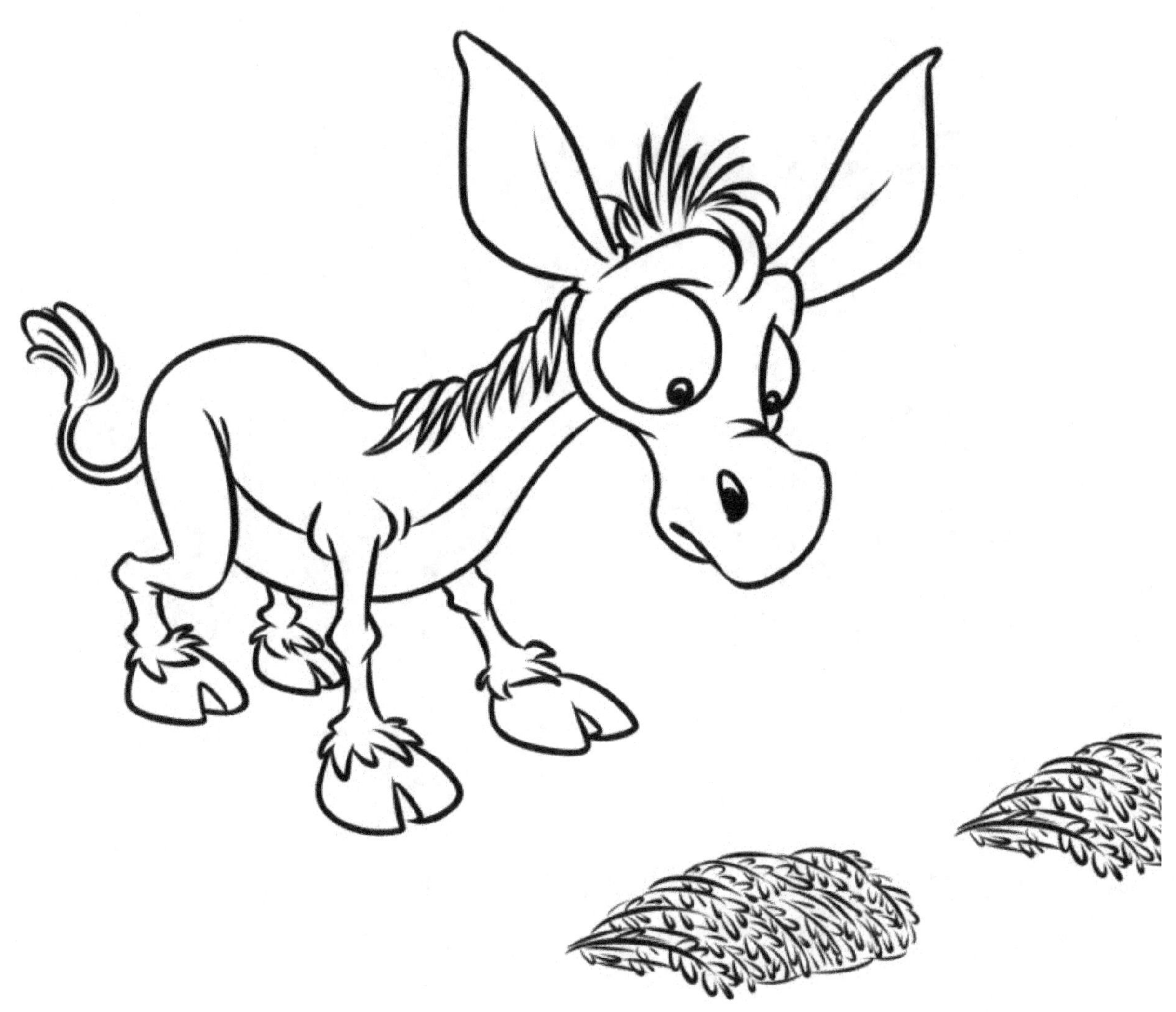

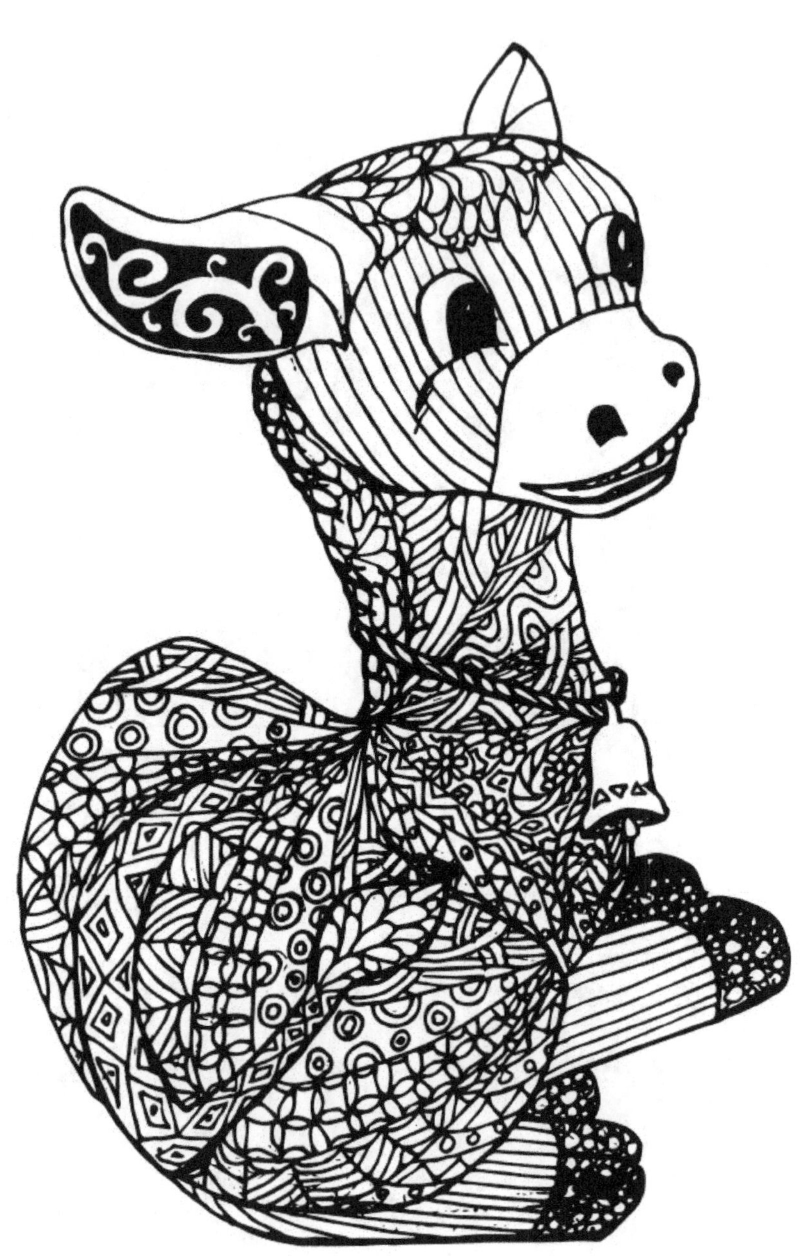

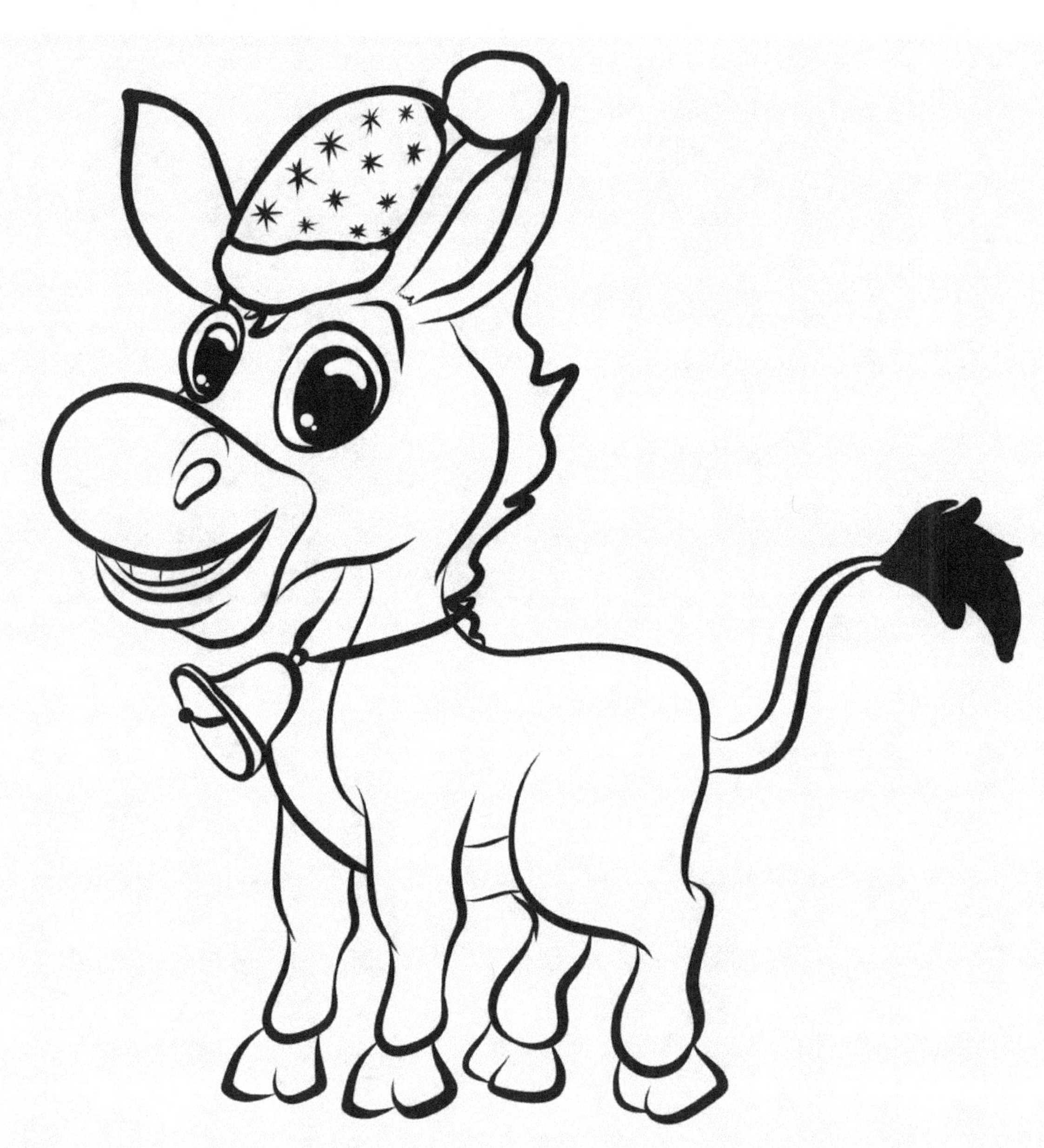

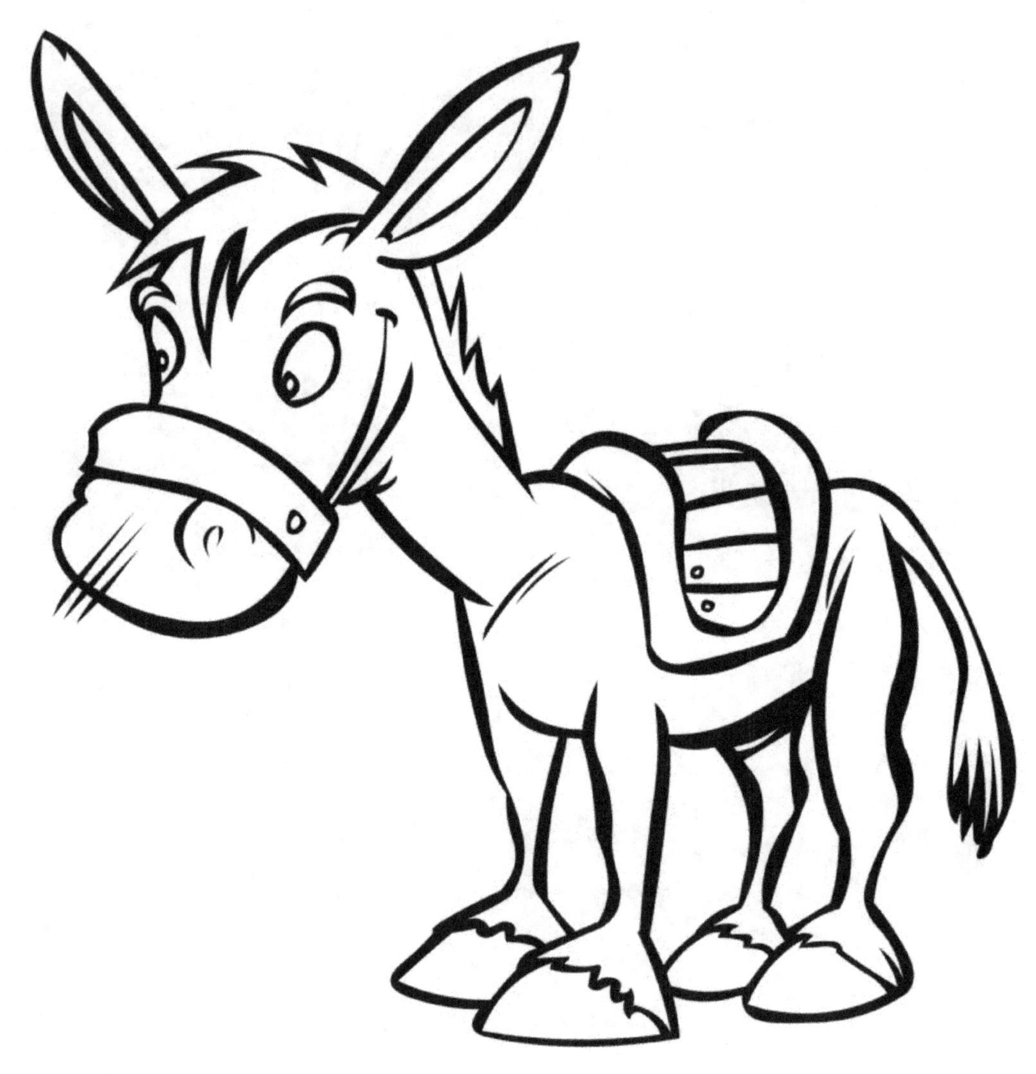